BY HIS STRIPES

BY HIS STRIPES

Hugh Jeter

GOSPEL PUBLISHING HOUSE
SPRINGFIELD, MISSOURI

02-0521

Library of Congress Catalog Card Number 76-20893

ISBN 0-88243-521-3

2nd printing 1979

Printed in the United States of America

Preface

When I was about 13 years old I suffered an accident while wrestling with another boy. I was taken to a doctor, and he determined that one rib was torn from the spine and another bent. The doctor bandaged me tightly and gave me strict instructions not to lift anything heavy, not to run, and so on. In a few days I fell and hurt myself anew. It was a long distance to a doctor—about a full day's trip. My father was a Presbyterian minister, and he decided that God could heal me. He reasoned that if God can answer prayer for one thing, He can also answer prayer for another—any answer to prayer is supernatural. He had proven repeatedly that God does answer prayer. He called together a group of believers and they prayed for me. I was instantly and completely healed. This was the beginning of my life-long interest in divine healing.

Some 50 years have passed since that time, and the Lord has been my "family physician" all these years. I can heartily recommend Him to all Christians. You cannot find a better physician.

During these intervening years I have had the privilege of sitting under the ministry of P. C. Nelson, Charles S. Price, Raymond T. Richey, Smith Wigglesworth, and many contemporary evangelists who have been used of God in praying for the sick. Many of these have been very close personal friends from whom I have received valuable lessons.

Being a foreign missionary for some 26 years and raising a family of five children (all of whom serve the Lord

5

6 BY HIS STRIPES

—four in fulltime missionary work), has given us many
occasions to prove the faithfulness of the One who is "a
very present help in trouble" (Psalm 46:1).

Besides working for the Lord on four continents and
some islands, I have had the privilege of visiting and
ministering in many countries of the world as well as my
assigned fields. This has given me an opportunity to
evaluate the role of divine healing on a much wider scale
than would have been possible otherwise.

Prayer for the sick has been a regular part of the services in the churches I have established or helped to
establish. It has also been my privilege to help in a
number of very large evangelistic campaigns on the mission field, where I have observed at close range the entire
operation, heard the testimonies of the healed, and seen
churches established as a result of these campaigns. In
some of these meetings I myself have been the evangelist
or one of the evangelists.

Returning from the mission field, I became an instruc-
tor at Southwestern Assemblies of God College, where I
have taught a two-semester hour course on divine healing
several times. This has served to intensify research on the
subject and to help formulate some definite concepts that
we believe to be completely Biblical as well as practical.

By His Stripes is an outgrowth of this background. God
grant that the truth presented here may be used to glorify
our wonderful Saviour and forward His cause throughout
the entire world.

HUGH P. JETER

Contents

Contents

1

The Nature of Divine Healing

Some years ago an extensive survey was made in the United States to find out what people want most. It was found that among the adults health was desired more than anything else. What good is accumulated wealth if you are too sick to enjoy it? With all the tremendous advances of medical science, disease still remains a number one problem. It is reported that in 1972, in the U.S., some 210,000 people died of cerebrovascular diseases, 346,000 of malignancies (73,000 from lung cancer alone), and 752,000 of diseases of the heart. In contrast to this, the total combat deaths of U.S. forces in Vietnam from 1961 to 1973 were less than 50,000. Which is the greater enemy—disease or war?

People are looking for an answer. They are desperate enough to try almost anything. The upsurge of new methods, new remedies, and new cults offering healing is evidence of this desire. Meanwhile, people generally ignore the Great Physician, the Creator, Jesus Christ himself. Doesn't it stand to reason that the man who makes a watch should know how to repair what he has made? Isn't it logical to believe that the One who made our physical bodies knows how to repair them?

What Divine Healing Is Not

First, let us clear away any false notions about divine healing.

9

It is not Christian Science. We neither deny the reality of matter nor pretend that everything depends entirely upon our thoughts. It is true that the mind has a great deal of power, and it is quite possible that illnesses that are psychosomatically induced can be alleviated by changing our thinking. Still, this type of healing has some very definite limitations.

It is not spiritism. We do not deny the existence of spirits—good or bad; however, the Bible in no place indicates that one should seek help from such spirits. Communication with the dead is forbidden in the Bible. (See Isaiah 8:19, 20; Deuteronomy 18:9-12; Exodus 22:18.) We are to put our trust in the living God, and not in a spirit pretending to be that of someone who has departed from this life.

It is not hypnotism, mesmerism, or magnetism. Admittedly, we do not understand some of the results produced by hypnotism, but I have never heard of a professional hypnotist who could cause the deaf to hear, the lame to be healed, and the blind to see. It is my understanding that the results of hypnotism are not permanent, but remain only while the subject is under the power of the hypnotic spell. Whatever power there may be in these methods cannot be classified as divine healing power, for many who practice hypnotism and the power of suggestion make no claim to a belief in God.

There are other methods that claim curative powers, but there is no need to mention all of them. Instead, let us look at what we believe to be genuine divine healing. If we have a clear understanding of this we will not be misled by false teachings and claims. We admit that there are counterfeits that deceive many people and bring reproach on the true gospel of healing. However, bear in mind that the devil will not waste time counterfeiting something that does not exist. Where there is a counterfeit, there must be the genuine. The genuine must also be of some worth. People don't go around counterfeiting pennies!

What Divine Healing Is

Divine healing is the process by which God supernaturally imparts life, health, and strength to afflicted souls and bodies.

In a sense, all physical healing is from God. The best physician on earth cannot heal a sick person if the body does not cooperate. It is not the doctor who heals. He merely helps your body to combat the illness. The defense and repair systems of our bodies are a continual source of amazement to those who are initiated into its secrets. These things were not invented by man, nor does he cause them to function. Many say that nature made us this way. We say that God made us this way. We do not understand nature to have mind, personality, intelligence, or emotions. We believe the laws of nature are simply the laws given by the great Creator of man and nature—God.

Thank God for the gradual healings that are brought about by the restorative powers God has placed within our physical bodies. Thank God for the means that speed up the natural processes of healing. We are most grateful for both. However, we wish to deal with the supernatural aspect of healing—the direct intervention of divine power that far supersedes the normal processes.

Let us first note that healing should not be thought of as something extraneous and entirely apart from our salvation. C. I. Scofield in his footnote on Romans 1:16 states: "The Hebrew and Greek words for salvation imply the ideas of *deliverance, safety, preservation, healing,* and *soundness.*" He calls salvation "the great inclusive word of the Gospel."[1] Healing and health are therefore included in the wonderful gift of God—salvation. Many are completely unaware of this and, as a result, do not receive the benefits provided for them in the Father's will (testament).

I like the idea of *soundness.* Divine healing is good, but I believe that a child of God can also enjoy divine health. This is based on the principle that it is better to build a fence at the top of a precipice than a hospital at the foot of it. A large percentage of our illnesses result from inner conflicts, worries, and emotions. (This will be discussed more fully in the next chapter.) Often it is impossible for the doctor to diagnose the real cause of the trouble. He has no medicine to cure the inner man, even if he is able to pinpoint the difficulty. Here is where the greatest of all physicians excels. He begins on the inside. He can heal the soul and change the very appetites and desires of the afflicted person. In fact, the apostle Paul tells us: "If any man be in Christ, he is a new creature [creation]: old things are passed away; behold, all things are become new" (2 Corinthians 5:17). Health is the natural result of such an inner transformation.

Purposes of Divine Healing

Many may question the importance of divine healing. What is the purpose behind it all? Since Jesus Christ spent such a large portion of the time during His ministry ministering to the sick and suffering, let us examine the record and try to find why He thought it so important.

Compassion loomed large in the healings performed by the Saviour. In Matthew 20:29-34 we read of the healing of two blind men. They called out for mercy (which is the same Greek word translated "compassion" in other references). He stopped and asked what they wanted. Was it a miracle of healing or only alms that they desired? They answered, "Lord, that our eyes may be opened." And the Scripture says, "So Jesus had compassion on them, and touched their eyes: and immediately their eyes received sight, and they followed Him" (v. 34). "Passion" carries the idea of "suffering." We speak of the Passion Week or the week of the sufferings of the Lord. The prefix *com* means "with." So *compassion* really means "to suffer with." If you really have compassion for a person it means you place yourself in his circumstances and feel his sorrow and his pain. This is a very important element if we wish to have success in praying for the sick. Somewhere I read:

> Lord, give me eyes that I might see,
> Lest I, as some folk will,
> Should pass by someone's Calvary
> And think it just a hill.

When the Lord met a funeral procession and knew that the young man who was deceased was the sole support— the only son—of a widow, the record says, "And when the Lord saw her, he had compassion on her, and said unto her, Weep not." He then gave the word of command, "And he that was dead sat up, and began to speak. And he delivered him to his mother" (Luke 7:11-15). How wonderful to know that our great High Priest is "touched with the feeling of our infirmities" (Hebrews 4:15).

Jesus healed, then, not just to show that He was the divine Son of God, but because He had mercy— compassion—on the people and wanted to help them. In fact, Christ did no miracles solely for His own benefit. His miracles always helped others. There was no self-seeking or desire to exhibit His supernatural powers simply to show what He could do.

Another purpose of the supernatural healing power demonstrated by Christ was to cause people to believe on Him and thus receive the gift of God, eternal life. Nicodemus was convinced. When he came to see Jesus and talk with Him, he began his remarks with: "Rabbi, we know that thou art a teacher come from God: for no man can do these miracles that thou doest, except God be with him" (John 3:2). Many Jews believed on Christ when Lazarus was raised from the dead. (See John 11:45; 12:10, 11.)

The healings of Christ attracted great crowds of people to hear His teachings and see the wonders that He performed. John 6:2 states: "A great multitude followed him, because they saw his miracles which he did on them that were diseased." Now, as then, the supernatural healing of the incurably sick attracts attention, and people will flock to the place where such things are taking place. The Psalmist put it this way: "O thou that hearest prayer, unto thee shall all flesh come" (Psalm 65:2).

The most important result of the healings performed by Christ was that God was glorified. The chief end of man is to glorify God. Therefore, we should seek things that will bring Him glory—things that will show how wonderful He really is. Look at a scene from the healing ministry of our Lord. In Matthew 15:30, 31 we read: "And great multitudes came unto him, having with them those that were lame, blind, dumb, maimed, and many others, and cast them down at Jesus' feet; and he healed them: insomuch that the multitude wondered, when they saw the dumb to speak, the maimed to be whole, the lame to walk, and the blind to see: and they glorified the God of Israel." When Christ laid His hands upon the woman who for 18 years had been so bound that she could not straighten up, the Bible says, "And immediately she was made straight, and glorified God" (Luke 13:13).

Some people seem to think that healing is from the devil. If so, he must have reformed! Since when did the devil begin to do things that bring glory to God?

When Jesus healed the man who had been born blind and then revealed to him that He was the Messiah, the man believed on Him and worshiped (John 9:38). In fact, after promising that those who believe on Him would do the same kind of works that He did, Jesus reinforced the statement with this promise: "And whatsoever ye shall ask in my name, that will I do, that the Father may be glorified in the Son" (John 14:13). There is no escaping the fact that this promise includes divine healing. Our answered prayers for the healing of the sick will bring glory to the God we serve.

One further motive for the healing of the sick in Christ's ministry was to enable the one who was healed to serve Him better. When Jesus went to Peter's house and found his mother-in-law sick with a fever, "He touched her hand, and the fever left her: and she arose, and ministered unto them" (Matthew 8:15). When the Lord cast out the legion of demons that had possessed the man of Gadara, he wanted to follow the Lord. But Jesus had another mission for him. He told him, "Go home to thy friends, and tell them how great things the Lord hath done for thee, and hath had compassion on thee" (Mark 5:19). What kind of a witness would he have been if he had not first been delivered by the power of God?

The Source of Divine Healing

One of the most important aspects of the doctrine of divine healing is to keep in mind the Source from which it comes. The Source is Jesus Christ himself. He said, "I am the way, the truth, and the life" (John 14:6). He also declared, with reference to His sheep (His people), "I am come that they might have life, and that they might have it more abundantly" (John 10:10). In his message to the people at the temple after the healing of the lame man, Peter called Christ "the Prince of life" (Acts 3:15). It is true that we receive our spiritual life by abiding in Him. It is equally true that He is the Source of physical life. "All things were made by him; and without him was not any thing made that was made" (John 1:3). Just to think that the Creator—the Author and Giver of life—can and will live His life in and through us! His radiant presence, the very source of light and life, will certainly bring life, strength, and health—abundant life—to His children that He loves so dearly!

Too many people make the mistake of seeking healing rather than the Healer. How would you feel if every time you went to see that "special person" you loved, she seemed far more interested in your gifts than in you? Healing should take a secondary role as we concentrate on getting better acquainted with the Healer.

For about 50 years I have known Jesus Christ as the Great Physician, and I would like to recommend Him to you. He is the best! Here are some of the reasons:

1. He is omniscient—all-knowing. He never makes a mistake in the diagnosis.
2. He is omnipresent. No matter where you are, He is at hand, ready, available.
3. He is omnipotent—all-powerful. There is nothing that He cannot do!
4. He is available to all. He will not turn down a new client. He invites your trust.

Christ's love and compassion are the same today as when He walked on this earth. His power has never diminished. All things are possible with Him. The One who said, "I am the Lord that healeth thee," is "Jesus Christ the same yesterday, and today, and for ever" (Hebrews 13:8).

I am the Lord, the God of all flesh: is there any thing too hard for me? Jeremiah 32:27

2

The God of the Supernatural

Basic to all belief in divine healing is the belief that God is supernatural. God must be supernatural or else He could not be God. If we believe in God as Creator, we most certainly believe He is supernatural.

Since God is supernatural, it is to be expected that He will work according to His nature. It is normal for God to do the supernatural.

Years ago, in Havana, I heard the well-known missionary and author, E. Stanley Jones, give the following illustration: "Suppose a man is walking down a path through the woods. Beside the path there is a toad underneath a stone. The toad wants to lift the stone, so he strains and bulges every muscle, but he cannot lift it. It is too big for him. The man comes along and easily picks up the stone, throwing it to one side. The toad looks up with surprise, blinks his eyes and croaks: 'A miracle!' A miracle for whom? It was a miracle for the toad because it was something he could not do. But it was only a normal thing for the man because he belonged to a different nature."

Nothing Too Hard for God

If we believe God is supernatural—omnipotent—then we should fully expect Him to do supernatural things. Opening blind eyes, causing the paralytic to walk and the dumb to speak may seem miraculous to us, but they are normal and natural for God. There is nothing too hard for Him. Most Christians today need to face squarely the

16

question Paul asked King Agrippa: "Why should it be thought a thing incredible with you, that God should raise the dead?" (Acts 26:8).

Perhaps, as J. B. Phillips suggests in the title of his book, *Your God is Too Small*. Of course, it is not God, but rather our concept of Him that is too small. We need a fresh glimpse of the God presented in the Holy Scriptures. The prophet Jeremiah declared: "Ah, Lord God! behold, thou hast made the heaven and the earth by thy great power and stretched out arm, and there is nothing too hard for thee" (Jeremiah 32:17).

Attitudes Toward Miracles

In the days of Jesus Christ's earthly life there were two main attitudes among the religious leaders regarding the miraculous. (1) The Sadducees, the "modernists" or "liberals" of their day, did not believe in angels, spirits, the resurrection, or any supernatural manifestations. (2) The Pharisees, the more "fundamentalist" type believed in miracles, angels, the resurrection, and so on. Yes, they believed in the miracles done in the days of Moses and those of their ancient past, but they would not accept the miracles of Jesus. They wanted to destroy any evidence of His miraculous power—such as Lazarus, whom He raised from the dead. They even plotted to kill Jesus.

The parallel is quite plain. These two philosophies still exist. Unfortunately, even among those who belong to churches that have divine healing as a part of their doctrine, there are many who believe in the miraculous healings of past years, but do not expect to see any today.

God's People and the Supernatural

The history of God's people has been a continual story of the supernatural. Look at the birth of Isaac. Humanly speaking, it was impossible for Sarah to bear a child at her advanced age. But as the angel told Mary, the mother of Jesus, when announcing that she was to conceive supernaturally, "With God nothing shall be impossible" (Luke 1:37).

Consider the call of Moses. As a prince in the house of Pharaoh, he had received the best education possible. Luke tells us, "Moses was learned in all the wisdom of the Egyptians, and was mighty in words and in deeds" (Acts 7:22). How did God get the attention of this highly educated individual? He used simply a burning bush in the desert; a bush that burned but was not consumed. The supernatural attracts people from all levels of society.

It took the supernatural to convince Moses that God really wanted him to attempt the liberation of the Children of Israel from their Egyptian bondage. After that it would certainly take miraculous signs to convince Pharaoh that he should free his slaves. Listen to what God told Moses: "Well do I know that the king of Egypt will not let you go, except by force. So I will exert my force and strike Egypt with all the marvels I intend to work there; after that he will let you go" (Exodus 3:19, 20, Moffatt). It is easy to see why the Egyptian king did not want to free his slaves. They did his work for him. They tilled his farms and built his cities, roads, and monuments. They even had a monetary value—they were his wealth!

Just for comparison, suppose you were the owner of a large cattle ranch. You have 10,000 head of white-faced beef cattle. One day a man comes to your house and announces solemnly: "I am a prophet of God. I have come to tell you that you should turn all those cattle loose and let them go." You would think that man was crazy! Pharaoh was not about to let his slaves go simply at the word of this man from the desert who called himself a prophet (i.e., one who speaks for God). It took force—the mighty hand of God displayed in a miraculous manner—to bring this hardhearted despot to his knees and compel him, even against his will, to let God's people go.

Now consider the parallel. Symbolically Egypt represents the world; Pharaoh—Satan; and slavery—the bondage of sin. Just as God has to have people through which He can carry out His work here in the world, Satan also enlists people to do his will. Christ tells us that those who sin are servants of sin (John 8:34). They are doing the devil's work. They are his slaves. He is a hardhearted taskmaster and absolutely will not let his slaves go free simply because you tell him that God sent you with this message. There are thousands of slaves of sin groaning beneath their tasks and longing for someone to deliver them. But it is going to take the supernatural power of God, the miraculous, to compel Satan to release them and bring about their liberation.

The Israelites really had something to talk about! They were told to tell their descendants about their experience. "Thou shalt say unto thy son, We were Pharaoh's bondmen in Egypt; and the Lord brought us out of Egypt with a mighty hand: and the Lord showed signs and wonders, great and sore, upon Egypt, upon Pharaoh, and upon all his household, before our eyes: and he brought us out from thence, that he might bring us in, to give us the land which he sware unto our fathers" (Deuteronomy 6:21-23). Undoubtedly the crossing of the Red Sea was one of the greatest miracles of history. Nothing is too hard for a God who can save His people in such an awesome manner.

If we believe the Biblical record of the Children of Israel in the wilderness, then we must believe in the miracle-working power of God. Think of a city with a population of 2 million people. How would you like to provide a week's supply of food for that many, especially in a desert with no source of supplies? Then there is the problem of water for such a multitude. Who of our modern engineers could contrive to bring the needed water from a rock? God did! We generally accept the account of God's provision for the Israelites in the wilderness at face value, and yet we wonder if God can supply the needs of our family of seven.

There were many other manifestations of the supernatural presence and power of the Lord during the wilderness journey, but we must hasten on. The crossing of the Jordan when it was at flood stage was the miracle that permitted the Israelites to first set foot on the soil of the Promised Land. The waters were held back by a supernatural force and they crossed over dry-shod. Imagine the effect the news of this crossing must have had on the inhabitants of the country!

The first great victory in the land was the taking of the city of Jericho. This was also made possible by an outstanding miracle. After carefully carrying out the detailed instructions given by God there was a triumphant shout of victory, the walls fell down, and the city was wide open to the invaders.

Joshua, Moses' chosen successor, led the Israelites from victory to victory in the conquest of Canaan. It seems that the Lord gave him special help in determining which course to pursue. The Book of Joshua is still studied by military strategists. Joshua's "long day" is an outstanding example of the supernatural help he received during this time. God's power turned slaves into conquerors!

After the period of conquest a sad note comes into the Biblical narrative. In Judges 2:7-11 we read: "And the people served the Lord all the days of Joshua, and all the days of the elders that outlived Joshua, who had seen all the great works of the Lord, that he did for Israel. And Joshua the son of Nun, the servant of the Lord, died. . . . And also all that generation were gathered unto their fathers: and there arose another generation after them, which knew not the Lord, nor yet the works which he had done for Israel. And the children of Israel did evil in the sight of the Lord, and served Baalim."

Do you see what happened? As long as the supernatural signs and wonders were being manifested the people followed the Lord. When the supernatural element ceased—when the people knew of the power of the Lord only as something historical or mere hearsay—they turned their backs on God and began to serve idols, gods of their own making. As long as religion is mere ritual and ceremonies or simply subscribing to a code of ethics, it is easy to change religions. After all, what's the difference? But it is difficult for a person to leave a religion where he has seen the supernatural power of God working. He can't deny what he has seen with his own eyes or experienced personally. You can't argue with facts—they are stubborn things!

Every generation needs to see the miraculous power of God manifested. This would prove to be a very effective antidote for some of the backsliding, skepticism, and apostasy of our days. Even second-generation Pentecostals who have never seen a miracle are in danger. How long has it been since a miracle has taken place in your church?

The beautiful song "How Great Thou Art" has found a responsive chord in the hearts of thousands of Christians today. Certainly the infinite, limitless scope of the wisdom, power, love, and grace of our God is indescribable. No wonder the Psalmist exclaims: "The heavens declare the glory of God; and the firmament showeth his handiwork" (Psalm 19:1). The universe plainly shows a guiding Intelligence that keeps everything in its proper course. The slightest variation in the orbits of planets would make such things as a "moon shot" impossible. Job says: "He stretcheth out the north over the empty place, and hangeth the earth upon nothing" (Job 26:7). It hangs all right, doesn't it? A God who can do that can do anything! The prophet Isaiah asks: "Who hath measured the waters in the hollow of his hand, and meted out heaven with the span, and comprehended the dust of the earth in a measure, and weighed the mountains in scales, and the hills in a balance?" (Isaiah 40:12). It is impossible for man to fully comprehend, much less describe, the greatness of our God.

Jesus Christ was God manifest in the flesh. He did the works of His Father. He stated: ". . . the works which the Father hath given me to finish, the same works that I do, bear witness of me, that the Father hath sent me" (John 5:36). His works were mighty, miraculous, supernatural; and the Father was pleased with the Son. The supernatural character of the ministry of Christ is evident throughout the New Testament. Not only did He heal the multitudes of every kind of sickness and disease —He cast out demons, caused paralytics to walk, and did many other miracles. If you just think for a moment, you will remember the turning of the water into wine, the feeding of the 5,000, the stilling of the tempest, walking on the water, the miraculous draught of fishes, and other nonhealing miracles. The whole point is this: If we believe that God is supernatural and that it is quite normal and natural for Him to do the supernatural, we have a basis for our belief in the power of the Lord to heal sin-sick souls and physical sicknesses today.

Certainly we must believe in the resurrection of Jesus Christ. Could there be a greater miracle than that? He said that no man took His life from Him, but that He had power to lay it down and power to take it up again. (See John 10:17, 18.) Paul states that Jesus was "declared to be the Son of God with power . . . by the resurrection from the dead" (Romans 1:4). If we believe the Bible, then we must believe that God is supernatural and that His Son, Jesus Christ, is also supernatural and able to do "exceeding abundantly above all that we ask or think" (Ephesians 3:20).

There are many in our world today who are searching for reality and are willing to abide by the decision, "The God that answereth by fire, let him be God" (1 Kings 18:24). Our God, the Creator of the heavens and the earth, was, is, and forever will be able to meet any challenge. There is nothing too hard for Him!

We can say today with the Psalmist: "You are the God of miracles and wonders! You still demonstrate your awesome power" (Psalm 77:14, *Living Bible*).

The blessing of the Lord, it maketh rich, and he addeth no sorrow
with it. Proverbs 10:22

3

Causes of Sickness

Where did sickness come from? How did it all get
started? Does God get glory from our suffering? If so,
should we try to get well?

During the days of the Spanish-American War, more
U.S. soldiers died in Cuba from yellow fever than from
enemy bullets. The trouble was that no one knew for sure
what caused the fever. There were many theories. Some
thought it was the water; others suggested that it was the
influence of the tropical moon. Some thought it must be
some food that caused the fever.

At last a young French-Cuban doctor educated in the
United States affirmed that the fever was transmitted by
the bite of a certain type of mosquito. The medical profession did not believe him and derided his theory. However, some medical officers of the U.S. Army carried out
further investigations and experiments and proved that
Carlos Finlay was right. When they knew the cause they
were able to exterminate the carrier of the disease and the
country was freed of this terrible scourge. During the 10
years we lived in Cuba, I don't recall hearing of a single
case of yellow fever.

This incident vividly illustrates the statement of the
Lord Jesus when He said: "Ye shall know the truth, and
the truth shall make you free" (John 8:32). We need to
know the truth about sickness and disease if we want to
be free from their power.

Recognizing the Enemy

It is important to recognize from the beginning the source of sickness. If a person believes that God has sent the sickness for some purpose, he may think he should not pray to be free from his affliction. (Although in most cases he will not hesitate to take medicine.) In Job 42:10 God referred to sickness as "captivity"; Jesus called it "bondage" (Luke 13:16); and the Holy Spirit called it "oppression" (Acts 10:38).

We cannot believe that God is the author of sickness and suffering. When He had finished all His creative work and inspected it, the result was: "And God saw everything that he had made, and, behold, it was very good" (Genesis 1:31). There was no sickness or physical imperfection in the garden of Eden until sin came into the picture. Even the tree of life was not forbidden to Adam and Eve until after the Fall. There is every indication that man would have lived indefinitely in his physical state if he had not sinned. It was not advisable to allow him to live forever in a sinful state, so God made other provisions for mankind.

Throughout the Bible there is a close association between sin and sickness. Sin and Satan are the indirect cause of all sickness, and sometimes the direct cause as well. Sin brought about physical death. Under the inspiration of the Holy Spirit, Paul declares that death is an enemy—the last enemy that will be put under the feet of our conquering Saviour (1 Corinthians 15:25, 26). If death is an enemy, then all that produces death or hastens its coming is also an enemy of the child of God. If sickness hastens death or incapacitates us from serving the Lord, then it is our enemy.

One of the greatest difficulties in the Korean War, and in Vietnam as well, was to be able to recognize the enemy. You can't just look at a man and tell whether he was born north or south of a certain parallel! We need to know whether sickness is from Satan or from the Lord, in order to take the necessary steps for deliverance.

The Works of the Devil

We realize that there are many natural causes of sickness and will deal with some of them later, but let us look first at the causes that are of a spiritual nature.

We know that Satan first brought sin into the world, and that sickness and death came as a result. In Job's case it is definitely stated that Satan was responsible for his physical affliction (Job 2:7). In Deuteronomy 28 we read of the many diseases that would come upon the Children of Israel if they failed to follow the Lord. Sickness was not considered a blessing, but a curse. In fact, the whole creation is still awaiting its release from the curse—the final redemption (Romans 8:22, 23).

Jesus said that the enemy comes to kill and destroy, but He came to give us abundant life (John 10:10). The wages of sin is death, but God's gift is life—eternal life (Romans 6:23). Jesus said that Satan had bound a certain woman for 18 years (Luke 13:16). He who came to "proclaim liberty to the captives" set her free from this bondage. We are told that Jesus came to "destroy the works of the devil" (1 John 3:8). He "destroyed" the diseases of all that came to Him. "How God anointed Jesus of Nazareth with the Holy Ghost and with power: who went about doing good, and healing all that were oppressed of the devil; for God was with him" (Acts 10:38). Remember, the devil oppresses. Christ sets free. If the sickness was the result of sin, Christ could both forgive the sin and remove the effect. He was not destroying the work of God but the work of the devil.

Many of the healings of our Lord were effected by rebuking a "spirit of infirmity" or casting out demons. (See Mark 9:22-29; Matthew 12:22; Luke 4:38, 39; 13:11; Mark 5:1-20.) If these sicknesses were from the Lord, surely He would not have employed this method.

Satan, the great deceiver, is supremely happy if he can so afflict a child of God that he is incapacitated and cannot wage active warfare against sin, and then cause him to believe that God has sent the affliction and he should not try to be freed from it. Let us not play into the hand of the enemy but rather resist him and share in Christ's victory.

It is important to remember that if the origin of the sickness is from some supernatural source, natural means will not effect the desired healing. The remedy must be through a superior spiritual power.

When God Allows Sickness

In the Bible we find that when God allowed sickness to come upon people and particular individuals, the reason was clearly implied or stated. A study of these incidents should help us avoid any similar affliction. I personally prefer preventive medicine rather than remedial measures.

Sickness was sometimes sent as judgment or punishment. Miriam was stricken with leprosy because she murmured against her younger brother, Moses. Jealousy was doubtless involved (Numbers 12:1-13). When Elisha's servant, Gehazi, coveted money and clothing he lied and deceived to obtain these things from Captain Naaman. His sin was discovered and he was smitten with leprosy (2 Kings 5:20-27). When the Israelites turned from God and worshiped a golden calf they had made, God sent a plague among them (Exodus 32:35). In the 28th chapter of Deuteronomy there is a long list of diseases that God said would come upon His children if they refused to obey Him and walk in His ways. A great number of the diseases that we are acquainted with today are included, but not one is called a blessing.

Sometimes sickness is allowed in order to arrest us and turn us from a wrong course. Perhaps we are too busy to learn some lessons any other way. In the 119th Psalm the author says: "Before I was afflicted I went astray: but now have I kept thy word." He then goes on to say: "It is good for me that I have been afflicted; that I might learn thy statutes" (vv. 67, 71). The infrequency with which this thought is found in God's Word may indicate that this is not His usual method of dealing with His children. It is true that God chastises His children at times (Hebrews 12:5-11); however, sickness is not the only method He uses.

There are incidents in the Bible when it seems that the Lord smote certain people as an example to others. Herod was smitten when he accepted the praise of those who said of his speech: "It is the voice of a god, and not of a man" (Acts 12:20-23). Ananias and Sapphira were stricken because they lied to the Holy Spirit. They pretended they had given all to God, but they had kept back something for themselves (Acts 5:1-11). Our Christian ranks today would be noticeably decreased if God struck down everyone who made false claims of surrender to Him.

The sin of irreverence is often overlooked, but it is no less sinful now than it was in olden days. The Children of Israel were told that they should not touch the ark of the covenant (Numbers 4:15). When some disobeyed, they were smitten (2 Samuel 6:6, 7; 1 Samuel 6:19, 20). When King Jeroboam stretched out his hand against the prophet of the Lord, his hand was paralyzed (1 Kings 13:4). When King Uzziah presumptuously acted as a priest and offered incense on the altar, he was smitten with leprosy (2 Chronicles 26:16-21). In his letter to the church at Corinth, Paul censured them for their irreverence. Seemingly, many were sick and others had died prematurely because they were irreverent at the Lord's table and had failed to discern the real significance of His sacrifice (1 Corinthians 11:20-22, 27-30). (Note that the word translated "unworthily" in verse 29 can also be translated "irreverently.")

Although in the final analysis sin is the cause of sickness and death, we must not conclude that sin is directly responsible in every case. Some have the tendency to think that the sick Christian must be guilty of some sin, or else he would not be sick. The disciples seemed to have this idea. A theological question was posed when they came upon a man born blind. "Who sinned, this man or his parents?" "How could he sin before he was born? or why should he suffer for another's sin?" They were interested in the theological implications. Jesus was interested in the man. Jesus answered them, "Neither hath this man sinned, nor his parents: but that the works of God should be made manifest in him" (John 9:3). We cannot always blame sin. There are many natural causes of sickness. We will now examine some of these.

Natural Causes of Sickness

We are told that our bodies are the temples of the Holy Spirit (1 Corinthians 6:19, 20). Surely we want to have God's temple clean and functioning as perfectly as possible. A Christian should, therefore, reject anything that would defile God's temple or impair his service for Him in any manner. Many of our illnesses are the result of improper care of our bodies. Wm. R. P. Emerson, M.D., suggests in his book *Health for the Having* that proper food and eating habits, fresh air and sunshine, exercise and rest are the essential elements for health.[1] We might add that cleanliness is also very important. Many diseases are contracted because of carelessness in hygiene.

God does not suspend the laws of nature for a person when he becomes a Christian. If he jumps off a high precipice, the law of gravity will apply to him and cause him to suffer the same as anyone else. If we abuse our bodies or fail to take proper care of them, we will suffer like other people. This means that we should use some common sense and cooperate with the laws of nature in order to have good health.

Even preachers are not exempt from natural laws. It is sometimes extremely difficult for them to get proper rest for their bodies. Sunday may be a day of rest for many, but it is a minister's busiest day. Many times they do not set aside 1 day in the week for rest, and therefore they violate the God-ordained principle that a man needs 1 day out of 7 for rest.

Intemperance has many forms. Someone has said that Americans dig their graves with their forks! Overweight is the big health problem in this land of plenty. Obesity—excess weight—is a very important factor in producing a heart condition. The number one killer in our country is diseases of the heart. It is said that mortality increases 1 percent with each pound of excess weight. Exercise is recommended almost unanimously by the medical profession for this problem. Even Paul recommended it in his day (1 Timothy 4:8). We should not neglect this important item.

Besides improper diet and lack of exercise, there are other things that are definitely harmful to the health. Alcoholism is one of the greatest problems faced today in many countries of the world. In Dr. S, I. McMillen's most interesting book *None of These Diseases*, he gives the following: "In the Journal of the American Medical Association, Milton Golin summarizes his article 'Robber of Five Million Brains' with the statement: 'Drink has taken five million men and women in the United States, taken them as a master takes slaves, and new acquisitions are going on at the rate of 200,000 a year.'"[2] The percentage of people being admitted into our mental institutions because of alcoholism is a very alarming figure. A few of the effects of alcohol directly related to health are: hardening of the liver; paralysis of certain muscles; neuritis; inflammation of the lining of the stomach; and cancer of the mouth, pharynx, larynx, esophagus, and liver. Recently the National Institute on Alcohol Abuse and Alcoholism reported that when heavy drinking and heavy smoking are combined, the risk of certain cancers is 15 times greater than among people who neither drink nor smoke.[3]

Since the report of the surgeon general on the harmful effects of cigarette smoking and its relation to cancer, a great amount of evidence has been accumulated on other injurious effects of smoking. Besides the well-established relationship of smoking to lung cancer, it now appears that smoking is a definite factor in many other diseases. The list is long, and growing constantly.

All who suffer because of the abuse of their bodies must certainly understand that they should repent of these abuses of the temple of the Spirit if they expect divine healing.

Sickness as a Result of Mental Stress
Besides all the causes of sickness already mentioned—and there are many more—we should turn our attention briefly to what is perhaps a major cause of sickness: emotional stress. Dr. McMillen quotes Dr. William Sadler as saying:

No one can appreciate so fully as a doctor the amazingly large percentage of human disease and suffering which is directly traceable to worry, fear, conflict, immorality, dissipation, and ignorance—to unwholesome thinking and unclean living. The sincere acceptance of the principles and teachings of Christ with respect to the life of mental peace and joy, the life of unselfish thought and clean living, would at once wipe out more than half the difficulties, diseases, and sorrows of the human race.[4]

There are various estimates as to the percentage of people suffering from sicknesses produced by emotional stress. Some doctors estimate that up to 80 percent of their patients would come under this category. It is a well-known fact that emotions such as anger, hatred, fear, and worry are very detrimental to health. This type of illness is very difficult for doctors to treat. For the most part they can only deal with the symptoms. Doctors can counsel and advise, but they cannot change the nature of the patient. Only God, our Great Physician, can do this!

Regardless of the cause of the illness, whether it is a result of accident, sin, abuse of our bodies, or emotional stress, God is abundantly able to deliver all those who put their trust in Him.

4

Healing in the Atonement

Whether or not physical healing was provided for the believer through the atoning death of Christ has been a subject of great controversy for many years. Let us try to look at the subject in an objective manner and find what the Bible really teaches.

A dictionary definition of the theological term *atonement* is as follows: "a) The redemptive work of Christ. b) The reconciliation between God and man effected by Christ's life, passion and death."[1]

Sin and sickness came as a result of the Fall. We know that the substitutionary death of Christ—the atonement —provided a means whereby God could forgive the sinner and yet be just. What about sickness? Was it included in the atonement? We believe that God provided a double remedy for the double curse. In Galatians 3:13 we read: "Christ hath redeemed us from the curse of the law, being made a curse for us: for it is written, Cursed is every one that hangeth on a tree." The redemption, then, was accomplished on the cross. He redeemed us from the curse of the Law.

The Law pronounced severe penalties or curses on those who refused to comply with the divine precepts. In Deuteronomy 28 there is a long list of diseases that would come upon those who refused to keep the law of God. In this case, at least, we see that sickness is a part of the curse. This agrees with the Biblical account of the fall of man and its consequences. How and where was the curse removed? By Christ's atoning death on the tree. Salvation was most certainly obtained at Calvary, and we have already noted that both the Hebrew and the Greek word for "salvation" includes the idea of "healing" and "soundness." This certainly seems to indicate that healing was included in the atonement. But there are other indications as well.

The Passover of the Jewish people was very significant. When the Lord was ready to deliver the Children of Israel from their bondage, they were given specific instructions how to celebrate the Passover. They were to take a lamb without blemish and kill it at the specified time. The blood was to be applied to the side posts and the lintel of the house. When the death angel came to a house where the blood was applied, he would "pass over" and not destroy the firstborn in that house (Exodus 12:1-13).

Paul tells us that "Christ our passover is sacrificed for us" (1 Corinthians 5:7). John the Baptist presented Christ to the world as "The Lamb of God, which taketh away the sin of the world" (John 1:29). So we believe that Christ was the antitype of the Passover lamb and died to set us free from the slavery of sin.

But a closer look reveals that not just the blood of the lamb was used. They were to roast the flesh and eat it to have physical strength for their journey. What physical benefits can be derived from the atonement of Christ? In Isaiah 53:5 we find the statement: "With his stripes we are healed." Can this mean physical healing or does it refer only to spiritual healing? A good translation of verse 4 would read like this: "Surely He hath borne our sicknesses and carried our pains." This undoubtedly refers to bodily ailments. For further confirmation of this, however, look at Matthew 8:16, 17. "When the even was come, they brought unto him many that were possessed with devils: and he cast out the spirits with his word, and healed all that were sick: that it might be fulfilled which was spoken by Isaiah the prophet, saying, Himself took our infirmities, and bare our sicknesses." Matthew definitely connects the physical healing of the sick with the atonement spoken of in Isaiah.

Going back to the first Passover we note that a remarkable occurrence must have taken place at the time. It seems that every individual that needed healing received it before the exodus from Egypt. They all *marched* out of the land, and Psalm 105:37 tells us, "There was not one feeble person among their tribes." There were doubtless no less than 1½ to 2 million of them, and "not one feeble person"! Where could we find that many people today without a sick person among them?

A genuine revival took place in the days of King Hezekiah. He was a good king, and exhorted the people to prepare themselves to seek the Lord. The people responded, and the Passover was kept. Hezekiah prayed for the people who really wanted to seek God but had not been able to comply with all the ceremonial rites of cleansing. The Lord answered his prayer. Second Chronicles 30:20 tells us: "And the Lord hearkened to Hezekiah, and healed the people." It was a time of great joy and rejoicing such as the land had not seen since the days of Solomon. Isn't it significant that they were healed when they partook of the Passover?

Speaking of His atoning death, Jesus said to Nicodemus: "As Moses lifted up the serpent in the wilderness, even so must the Son of man be lifted up" (John 3:14). You will recall that the Children of Israel were in the wilderness. God was providing for all their needs, but they were not satisfied with His provision. They began to complain that there was neither bread nor water, and they were tired of the manna that the Lord supplied. They murmured and complained against Moses and against God. As a result, the Lord sent fiery serpents among them. These serpents bit the people and many of them died. They then acknowledged their sin and asked forgiveness. God instructed Moses to make a serpent of brass and put it up on a pole where all could see it. Those who looked at the serpent of brass were cured, and those who did not look perished (Numbers 21:4-9).

This has always been understood to be a type of Christ and His redemptive work on the cross. As such, we should be aware of the fact that physical healing was a part of the type and should be included in the antitype as well. "Life for a look at the Crucified One"—spiritual life, and physical life as well.

A type of the atonement is also found in Leviticus 13 and 14 where it tells of the cleansing of the lepers and the sacrifices prescribed. The atonement had to be made with blood, and although leprosy is a type of sin, physical healing was definitely involved.

Now let us take a more detailed look at the great chapter of the suffering Messiah—Isaiah 53. Isaiah 53:4 reads: "Surely he hath borne our griefs, and carried our sorrows." Many scholars have pointed out that the word for "grief" (Hebrew, *Kholee*) is generally translated "sickness" and is from the word *chalah*—to be weak, sick, or afflicted. In other passages in the Old Testament it is translated "sickness." Also, the word *sorrows* (Hebrew, *makob*) is translated "pain" in Job 33:19 and Jeremiah 51:8. The version given in Matthew 8:17 ("Himself took our infirmities, and bare our sicknesses") is therefore a far more accurate translation.

It has also been pointed out that the two verbs employed here are significant. In the first case, the Hebrew *nasa* ("He hath borne") is the same verb that is used in Isaiah 53:12 where we read: "He bare the sin of many." Christ bore our sins by suffering vicariously in our place. If this is true of our sins, then it must be equally true of our sicknesses, for the same verb is used to describe the action.

Then the second verb *carried* (Hebrew, *cabal*) can also have the meaning of "bearing something as a penalty." In verse 11, we read: "For he shall bear [*cabal*] their iniquities." In both instances, then, the same Hebrew verbs are used for bearing (or carrying away) both our sins and our sicknesses. Praise God! How could it be plainer?

The logical conclusion is this: If Christ bore the penalty for my sins, then I do not have to bear it. If Christ bore my sicknesses, then I do not have to suffer them. His sacrifice was complete, nothing lacking.

Let us now turn our attention to a statement found in verse 5: ". . . and with his stripes we are healed." The first part of the verse says that He was wounded for our transgressions and bruised for our iniquities. No Bible-believing Christian would deny the present-day application and efficacy of Christ's suffering for our sins. Why, then, would anyone doubt for a moment that the healing He purchased for us is no longer available or no longer efficacious? A seeker of salvation could easily say to a Christian worker who did not believe in divine healing, "If you say that we are no longer healed by His stripes, how do I know that I can be cleansed by His blood?"

Think with me, if you will, of the terrible scourging that Christ went through before He ever went to the cross. The shorthandled whip that often had lacerating objects fastened to the leather thongs was brought down with strength, and oftentimes with fury, on the bared back of the victim. The Jews had a law that did not permit them to administer more than 39 lashes. The Romans had no such law. Some of those who were flogged by the Roman soldiers died under the severity of the beating and did not go to the cross. No doubt these soldiers would relish the opportunity to vent their fury on a hated Jew, especially one who claimed to be a king!

Dr. T. J. McCrossan points out that in 1 Peter 2:24 the word that is translated "stripes" is literally "bruise." He stresses the fact that it is singular and not plural, meaning that the entire back of the Lord was like one big bruise.[2] Surely God, as a merciful and loving Father, would not allow His Son to undergo such excruciating suffering if it were not necessary. What was the purpose? The atonement for our *sins* was effected on the cross. "With his stripes we are *healed*." Healing for our bodies, as well as healing for our souls, was provided by our Lord through His atoning death.

Notice also that Peter, looking back at the accomplished work of Calvary, says: "By whose stripes ye *were* healed" (1 Peter 2:24). Christ does not have to suffer again to provide forgiveness of sin or healing of the sick. The work has already been done. It is now up to us to accept the finished work of Christ and appropriate by faith the forgiveness or healing that we need.

In writing to the church at Corinth about the observance of the Lord's Supper, or Communion, Paul first enumerates some of the weaknesses and sins that were present among the believers. Then he tells them: "For this cause many are weak and sickly among you, and many sleep"(1 Corinthians 11:30). When we partake of the Communion, we take both the bread and the fruit of the vine. We know that the fruit of the vine represents the blood of the Lord that was shed for the remission of sin, but what does the bread represent? We know, of course, that it represents the body of the Lord. We refer to the "broken body," but is it possible that we do not discern the full significance of His body? Are there benefits to be derived from that body that we fail to obtain simply because we are unaware of them? If so, the same thing could happen to us as happened to the church at Corinth. Many could be sickly and others could die prematurely.

The Psalmist exhorts: "Bless the Lord, O my soul, and forget not all his benefits: who forgiveth all thine iniquities; who healeth all thy diseases" (Psalm 103:2, 3). Physical healing is one of the benefits our wonderful Lord has provided for His own. It has been bought and paid for, yet many of His dear children have forgotten this most important benefit.

Many cases could be cited of those who have been instantly healed while taking Communion. Moffatt's translation of Isaiah 53:5 says: "The blows that fell to him have brought us healing." Let us not forget this benefit. The atonement was complete, not partial. Don't fail to get the full benefit provided by our Lord at such an awful cost! Satan has no right to lay on us that which has already been laid on Christ. When he tries to do so, resist him with the sword of the Spirit, the Word of God. The atonement of Christ makes possible our redemption. We are redeemed from the curse of both sin and sickness.

There are seven names of Jehovah called the Seven Redemptive Names of our Lord. These names reveal the character and work of Christ. We certainly accept "The Lord our Righteousness," "The Lord our Shepherd," and four of the other names, applying them to ourselves and claiming the blessings revealed through His name. However, we sometimes fail to realize that among these redemptive names is "The Lord our Healer" (Jehovah-Rapha). Should we not acknowledge this important characteristic of our Lord? He never changes.

I once heard an evangelist tell of a poor European who wanted to immigrate to the United States. After some years of saving his money, he was able to get enough together to pay for steerage passage on a ship bound for America. He took along with him some food that would not spoil during the trip. While the other passengers were eating in the dining room, he would go off by himself and eat his crackers and cheese. Near the end of the trip he was so tired of this fare and the smells from the dining room were so tempting, that he got up the courage to ask one of the ship's stewards how much it would cost to get a warm meal. The steward looked at him and said, "You have your ticket, don't you?" "Yes," the man answered. "Well, your meals are all included in the price of your ticket." Think of all this poor man had missed simply because he didn't know of the benefit that was his, that had already been bought and paid for! Let us not overlook any of the benefits our Lord has purchased for us.

5

Old Testament Healings

It has been said that the past should be used as a guide to the future. On this basis, let us look at the record to see if God has healed in the past, who He has healed, and under what circumstances or conditions. The next few chapters will be given to this research.

The Healing of Job

Most scholars agree that the Book of Job is probably the oldest book of the Bible. If so, the healing of Job would be the first recorded healing in the Bible. Job was a good man. God himself said so. In fact, God wasn't afraid to hold him up as an example of uprightness even to the devil himself. Satan, who is called the "accuser" (Revelation 12:10), characteristically began to falsely accuse Job, saying that he served God only for personal benefit. God then permitted Satan to afflict Job. First he stripped him of his wealth and his family in one blow. Job remained faithful to his God. Then the devil was allowed to smite Job with severe boils all over his body. It is almost impossible to imagine the pain and suffering he went through. Think of standing, sitting, and lying on boils. Even Job's wife told him, "Dost thou still retain thine integrity? curse God, and die" (Job 2:9). Job did not know why he was being tested. He thought it was God himself who was afflicting him. Nevertheless he said, "I know that my Redeemer liveth" (Job 19:25). When Satan had done his best and failed, God again took charge. He reproved Job's friends and told them to repent and Job would pray for them. God "turned the captivity of Job, when he prayed for his friends." God healed him and restored his former prosperity, even giving him double what he had before (42:10-12).

Many books have been written about Job, but we will note here only a few things that seem important in relation to his healing. Notice first that it was Satan who afflicted him. God allowed him to do so for a purpose, but God is not the author of sickness. Second, God called this loathsome disease "captivity." It was not classified as a divine blessing or favor of the Lord. Third, Job knew that somewhere there was a Redeemer. His cry was, "Oh that I knew where I might find him!" (Job 23:3). There are many people today who are suffering. They know that somewhere there is a Redeemer, but they don't know where to find Him. Fourth, Job was healed when he got his eyes off his own troubles and prayed for others.

Health and Healing During the Exodus

When the Israelites made their exodus from Egyptian bondage, it is recorded that "there was not one feeble person among their tribes" (Psalm 105:37). This was beyond doubt the greatest mass healing in all history. To these newly enfranchised people the Passover represented redemption—deliverance of both soul and body.

God's concern for the health and well-being of His people was demonstrated in the laws of sanitation that He gave to Moses. The sanitation of the camp is described in Deuteronomy 23:12, 13. Segregation of the leper was commanded in Leviticus 13. This was some 2500 years before medical science determined that this was the basic step toward the eradication of leprosy and other contagious diseases. Cleansing of the body and changing of clothes were stressed in Numbers 19. All in all, it can be said that the sanitary laws God gave His people were excellent and far ahead of anything that was known by the medical profession of those days.

Aaron and Miriam spoke against Moses because they didn't like the wife he had chosen. There was doubtless some racial prejudice involved. Then too, it may simply have been "in-law" trouble. There also seems to have been some jealousy because their younger brother had risen to such prominence and was being blessed of the Lord. God heard their complaints and called them to task for it. Miriam was stricken with leprosy. There was quick repentance. Aaron begged Moses to have mercy. Moses prayed for Miriam and the Lord healed her, although she had to remain outside the camp for 7 days. They could not travel until she was taken back into the camp (Numbers 12).

God does not strike people with leprosy today when they complain against their spiritual leaders, but He has shown His attitude toward this sin. They had to repent before they could receive their healing. Moses (the meekest man on earth, v.3) was willing to forgive this personal affront committed by his own brother and sister, and pray earnestly for Miriam's recovery. Note also that the progress of the entire multitude was hindered by the sin of these two individuals.

After the triumphant crossing of the Red Sea and the destruction of their enemies, the Israelites faced one of the first crises of their wilderness journeys. They found water, but it was too bitter to drink. Moses interceded for the people, and the Lord healed the waters. It was there that the Lord made a convenant with His people. He told them: "If thou wilt diligently hearken to the voice of the Lord thy God, and wilt do that which is right in his sight, and wilt give ear to his commandments, and keep all his statutes, I will put none of these diseases upon thee, which I have brought upon the Egyptians: for I am the Lord that healeth thee" (Exodus 15:26).

Several important things are brought out in this verse. First, the lord here declares himself for the first time as a physician or healer. "The Lord that healeth thee," is the translation of "Jehovah-Rapha," one of the redemptive names of the Lord. This title clearly indicates something of the nature, ability, and willingness of our Lord to heal the sick. This could well be translated, "I am the Lord thy Physician." Certainly no finer physician can be found than the One who created us!

Second, we should note that this was a covenant—a

pact—that God made with His people. It was not some "off-the-cuff" remark, but a solemn promise that became a sacred obligation. God is always faithful to His promises.

Third, the promise was conditional. They were to keep His commandments, listen diligently to His voice, and do what was right. Then, and only then, would the Lord be obligated to keep His part of the contract. This convenant of healing and health has never been rescinded. It is valid today.

The Book of Deuteronomy contains a repetition of many of the most important items of the Law given in the previous books of Moses. It is not surprising, therefore, to find the healing covenant repeated in chapter 7. Beginning with verse 12, the people are reminded of their part of the pact. They are told that if they keep the law of the Lord, He will surely respect the covenant He has made with them. They are then told of some of the blessings that would be theirs as a result of their obedience. Among these blessings we read in verse 15: "And the Lord will take away from thee all sickness, and will put none of the evil diseases of Egypt, which thou knowest, upon thee; but will lay them upon all them that hate thee." This was a definite reaffirmation of the previous pact.

The promise of healing and health was conditional upon the obedience of God's people to the conditions He had given them. No doctor can guarantee results if you do not follow his directions. The Israelites did not follow the Lord at all times as they should have. In Numbers 21 we read the story of the complaining and murmuring of the Israelites against Moses and against God. Some people seem to value security more than freedom. God was displeased with their grumbling and sent fiery serpents among them. Many were bitten and died. Then the Israelites repented, Moses prayed, and God provided a remedy. Those who accepted the remedy God provided were healed.

Looking once more at the convenant of healing in Exodus 15:26 we find it quite evident that health, as well as healing, was involved. This is further confirmed by Exodus 23:25: "And ye shall serve the Lord your God, and he shall bless thy bread, and thy water; and I will take sickness away from the midst of thee." This sounds good! I much prefer health to healing. Years ago I read of a country where the families paid their doctor as long as all were in good health. As soon as any member of the family became sick, payments to the doctor were discontinued until that person was well again. Sometimes I wonder if we are following the wrong system.

The One who told the Israelites that He was their Physician said that He would take all sickness away from them. That was a tremendous promise. Was He able to do it? Read again Psalm 105:37: "He brought them forth also with silver and gold: and there was not one feeble person among their tribes." Hallelujah! He is able!

God's Life Insurance

Almost everyone is interested in life insurance. Are you familiar with God's life insurance plan? It has always seemed a bit strange to me that life insurance does not insure your life! It cannot assure you of even 1 year of additional life. It can only offer to pay or give some form of assistance to those who are left behind when you die. God can and does guarantee long life on certain conditions. In the Ten Commandments we read: "Honor thy father and thy mother: that thy days may be long upon the land which the Lord thy God giveth thee" (Exodus 20:12). This promise is reaffirmed in the New Testament. In Ephesians 6:1-3 we find: "Children, obey your parents in the Lord: for this is right. Honor thy father and mother; which is the first commandment with promise; that it may be well with thee, and thou mayest live long on the earth." This is life itself, promised by the Author of life. A similar promise of life is found in the 34th Psalm: "What man is he that desireth life, and loveth many days, that he may see good? Keep thy tongue from evil, and thy lips from speaking guile. Depart from evil, and do good; seek peace, and pursue it" (vv. 12-14). This passage is repeated, almost verbatim, in 1 Peter 3:10, 11.

Hezekiah's Healing

Hezekiah, the king, was sick and about to die. In fact, the prophet had told him to set his house in order for it was now his time to go. He had been a good king and had not only served God himself but had also turned many of his people back to God. When he was told that he would die, he began to pray to God and weep. He reminded the Lord that he had followed Him faithfully. The Lord heard his prayer, and Isaiah the prophet was told to return and give him a new message. He would not die, but would have 15 years added to his life. He was given a sign—the shadow on the sundial went back 10 degrees—something that had never happened before or since (2 Kings 20:1-11).

Notice that in this case sin was not the cause of Hezekiah's sickness; he was faithfully serving the Lord. It is also noteworthy that it was not the prayers of the prophet that brought an answer, but Hezekiah's own prayers.

The Healing of Naaman

A most remarkable healing is narrated in 2 Kings 5. Naaman was a high-ranking officer in the Syrian army. He was a close friend of the king and a national hero, but he was a leper. A little Hebrew slave girl who worked for Naaman's wife told them that there was a prophet in Israel who could heal his leprosy. With the king's approval Naaman made the journey. He was quite upset and left in a rage when the prophet didn't come out to greet him and perform some type of religious ritual over him for his healing. However, he showed his true greatness by being willing to listen to the advice of one of his servants. Following the prophet's instructions he went to the Jordan River, washed seven times, and was healed.

From this story we learn (1) that God showed mercy and healed one who was not an Israelite, (2) that strict obedience is a condition for receiving the blessing of God, (3) that one must be willing to humble himself, and (4) that nothing is impossible with God. Through this healing Naaman was convinced that Jehovah is the only true God, and he vowed that he would never again worship any other god.

Other Old Testament Examples

Elisha was used of God to restore to life the son of the

Shunammite woman (2 Kings 4:8-37). David probably experienced more than one healing from the Lord. In Psalm 30:2, 3 he says: "O Lord my God, I cried unto thee, and thou hast healed me. O Lord, thou hast brought up my soul from the grave: thou hast kept me alive, that I should not go down to the pit." He also exhorts us not to forget any of the benefits of the Lord and lists healing as one of them (Psalm 103:1-5). There are a number of other healings mentioned in the Old Testament, but those cited are sufficient evidence that God did heal His people in those ancient times.

In contrast to those who sought God in their affliction and were healed, we have the case of King Ahaziah of Israel. He had a fall, so he sent messengers to Ekron to inquire of their god Baal-zebub if he would recover or not. An angel of the Lord told Elijah to meet the messengers and send them back to their master. They were to tell him that he would surely die because he had not sought the true God but had sent to inquire of the pagan deity "the god of flies." He died according to the word of the Lord (2 Kings 1:2-17).

Asa was a very good king during most of his 41-year rule. Toward the end of his reign he depended on help from the king of Syria, and the prophet Hanani was sent to reprove him for this evident lack of trust in God. Asa became angry and ordered the prophet to be placed in prison. After this he had a very severe disease in his feet. The Scripture tells us, "His disease was exceeding great: yet in his disease he sought not to the Lord, but to the physicians" (2 Chronicles 16:12). He doubtless knew that if he expected to get any answer from the Lord he would have to repent and ask forgiveness. This he did not want to do, so he had to take the consequence—death.

There is very little mention of physicians in the Bible. It is possible that in Asa's day they were more of the magician or medicine-man type. Seeking divine healing requires heart-searching on the part of the sick person, which results in real spiritual benefit.

At the dedication of Solomon's Temple God promised He would heal their land (2 Chronicles 7:14). This, no doubt, included the people as well as the land itself. On the evidence of the cases cited there can be no doubt that God healed in Old Testament times. He tells us, "I am the Lord, I change not" (Malachi 3:6).

God has revealed himself as the Great Physician. He has covenanted to heal His people. He has given us sufficient evidence of His miraculous power. He invites us: "Call upon me in the day of trouble: I will deliver thee, and thou shalt glorify me" (Psalm 50:15). We are exhorted not to forget any of His benefits. Let us pray with the prophet Jeremiah: "Heal me, O Lord, and I shall be healed; save me, and I shall be saved: for thou art my praise" (Jeremiah 17:14).

6

The Healing Ministry of Christ

The earthly ministry of the Lord Jesus Christ was threefold. This is clear from the above verse and also from Matthew 4:23: "And Jesus went about all Galilee, *teaching* in their synagogues, and *preaching* the gospel of the kingdom, and *healing* all manner of sickness and all manner of disease among the people." Many of the followers of the Lord today stress the *teaching* and the *preaching,* but believe that the *healing* ministry is only for those who have received special powers from the Lord. Others think it should be left entirely to the medical profession.

When Christ was on earth no one attempted to deny His healing power, but some religious leaders seriously questioned His authority to forgive sins. Today religious leaders in general do not question the authority of the Lord to forgive sins, but many of them seem to question His power to heal the sick. In all fairness we should say that the Lord presented in His ministry indisputable evidence of the healing of the sick, and many of our leaders today have not seen that same kind of evidence. Unfortunately, many are looking for evidence to prove that Christ does not heal. They search for evidence to bolster their theories, instead of searching for the truth.

Physical healing played a very important part in the ministry of our Lord. It would be difficult to estimate what percentage of His time was spent ministering to the sick. John says, "And a great multitude followed him, because they saw his miracles which he did on them that were diseased" (John 6:2). So many sought Him for His healing ministry that at times "they had no leisure so much as to eat" (Mark 6:31). The first recorded message of our Lord tells us that He came "to heal the brokenhearted, to preach deliverance to the captives, and recovering of sight to the blind" (Luke 4:18). He also said that the Spirit had anointed Him for that purpose. This was reaffirmed by Peter when he was preaching at Cornelius' house. "How God anointed Jesus of Nazareth with the Holy Ghost and with power: who went about doing good, and healing all that were oppressed of the devil; for God was with him" (Acts 10:38). The healing of the sick was a definite part of Christ's ministry, and He healed through the power of the Holy Spirit.

What Kind of Healings Did the Lord Perform?

We live in an age of specialization. Did the Lord heal only certain types of diseases? A partial list of the healings of the Lord includes the following:

Blindness	Matthew 12:22; 15:30; 21:14; Mark 10:46-52; Luke 7:21.
Deafness	Mark 9:25-27; Matthew 11:5.
Demon possession	(Note: When the Scriptures refer to "devils" it is to be interpreted "demons." There is one devil, but many demons.) Matthew 4:24; 8:16; 8:28-34; 9:32, 33; 12:22; 15:22-28; 17:18; Mark 1:32-34, 39; 7:26-30; 16:9; Luke 4:41; 8:2, 26-36; 9:42; 11:14; 13:32.
Dropsy	Luke 14:2-4.
Dumbness	Matthew 12:22; 15:30; Mark 9:17-27.
Ear restored	Luke 22:51.
Fever	Matthew 8:14, 15.
Hemorrhage	Mark 5:25, 29; Luke 8:43-48.
Hunchback	Luke 13:11-13.
Impotency	John 5:5-9.
Lameness	Matthew 15:30; 21:14.
Leprosy	Matthew 8:2, 3; Luke 5:12, 13; 17:12-14.
Lunacy	Matthew 4:24.
Maimed	Matthew 15:30, 31.
Palsy	Matthew 4:24; Matthew 8:5-13; 9:2-7;

Luke 5:18-25; Mark 2:3-12.

Spirit of infirmity	Luke 13:11-13.
Terminal illness	Luke 7:2-10.
Unclean spirits	Mark 1:23-26; 5:2-15; 7:25-30; Luke 4:33-36; 6:18; 8:26-35; 9:42.
Withered arm	Matthew 12:10-13.

Besides the individual cases of healing mentioned, it is also recorded that the Lord healed:

Many	Mark 1:34; 3:10; Luke 7:21.
Divers diseases	Matthew 4:24; Mark 1:34; Luke 4:40.
Multitudes	Matthew 12:15; 19:2; Luke 5:15; 6:17-19.
All that were sick	Matthew 8:16; 12:15; 14:14; Luke 4:40; 6:19; 9:11.

In one case, due to the unbelief of the people, it is stated that "He laid His hands upon *a few sick folk*, and healed them" (Mark 6:5).

The One who said, "I am the resurrection, and the life" (John 11:25), proved that this was no idle boast by actually raising to life those who were dead. There are three recorded cases of Christ's raising the dead: (1) The daughter of Jairus, Mark 5:22-43; (2) The son of the widow of Nain, Luke 7:11-15; (3) Lazarus, John 11:1-44.

The Gospels do not record all the healings that our Lord performed. The apostle John says: "And many other signs truly did Jesus in the presence of his disciples, which are not written in this book" (John 20:30). He also states: "And there are also many other things which Jesus did, the which, if they should be written every one, I suppose that even the world itself could not contain the books that should be written" (John 21:25). This shows that we have only a partial record of the great healings, signs, and wonders that our Lord performed during the short 3½ years of His earthly ministry. However, enough instances are cited to show (1) that the Lord was deeply concerned with physical healing, (2) that He dedicated a large part of His time to this ministry, and (3) that every kind of disease was subject to His healing power.

Many people admit that Christ heals some people but

are in doubt as to who He will heal. In the accounts cited above we see that He healed Jews and Gentiles, Pharisees and publicans, saints and sinners. He healed all who came to Him for healing. True, all did not follow Him afterward, but they had a testimony of the power of God which they would never forget and which would confront them on the day of judgment.

Why Did Christ Heal?

1) *To show compassion.* Many Scripture passages indicate the infinite compassion of our Lord. It is a part of His nature. Many are moved or motivated to do things because of jealousy, envy, hatred, or fear. Jesus was not moved by any such emotions, but many times in the Scriptures we are told He was moved by compassion. The following passages are instances where it is clearly indicated that the Lord was moved with compassion and healed the sick: Matthew 14:14; 20:34; Mark 1:40, 41; 5:19; 9:22; Luke 7:13.

2) *To fulfill prophecy.* When the crowd gathered at Peter's house after the healing of his mother-in-law, the Lord healed them all. Matthew tells us that He did this "that it might be fulfilled which was spoken by Isaiah the prophet, saying, Himself took our infirmities, and bare our sicknesses" (Matthew 8:17).

3) *To prove God had sent Him.* Peter told the people on the Day of Pentecost that Jesus of Nazareth had been approved of God among them by miracles and wonders and signs, which God did by Him (Acts 2:22). John the Baptist was an outstanding servant of God and he bore witness to the fact that Jesus was indeed the Son of God (John 1:34). But Jesus said that there was still a more powerful witness. Listen to His words: "But I have greater witness than that of John: for the works which the Father hath given me to finish, the same works that I do, bear witness of me, that the Father hath sent me" (John 5:36). He also said: "The works that I do in my Father's name, they bear witness of me" (John 10:25). He even seemed to indicate that it would not be a sin to disbelieve Him if He did not produce supernatural evidence of His divine origin. "If I had not done among them the works

which none other man did, they had not had sin" (John 15:24). (Remember that all through John's Gospel he uses the word *works* to refer to divine healings and other supernatural manifestations.)

4) *To enable the healed to minister.* As soon as Peter's mother-in-law was healed she arose and ministered to them (Matthew 8:14, 15). When the Gadarene demoniac was healed he was sent to witness to his countrymen (Mark 5:18-20).

5) *To impart more abundant life.* He plainly declared, "I am come that they might have life, and that they might have it more abundantly" (John 10:10). He is the Source of life (John 14:6; 1:4). He came to give us eternal life (John 3:16). We receive this life as we remain in Him (John 15:4; 1 John 5:11, 12).

6) *To destroy the works of the devil.* Satan, the devil, is to blame for bringing into this world both sin and sickness. Christ came to destroy the works of the devil (1 John 3:8). He did not do a halfway job! Those who believe on Him can already enjoy the fruits of His victory, and eventually Christ will put an end to all sin, sickness, and death (Revelation 21:4, 27; 1 Corinthians 15:26).

7) *To manifest the works of God.* When the disciples questioned Jesus as to whose sin was responsible for a certain man's blindness, Jesus said: "Neither hath this man sinned, nor his parents: but that the works of God should be made manifest in him" (John 9:3). The results of many of the healings performed by Christ were that the people wondered and glorified God. (See: Matthew 9:8; 15:31; Mark 2:12; Luke 5:26; 7:16; 13:13; 17:15.)

How Did Christ Heal?

A careful study of the Scriptures leads many to believe that Christ did not heal by His own power, as the divine Son of God, but through the power of the Holy Spirit (Luke 4:14, 18; John 5:19; Acts 10:38). This could be because He did not want to use a power that would not be available to His followers. Some of the ways in which Christ healed are as follows:

1) He laid hands on the sick and healed them (Mark 5:23; 6:5; 8:23; Luke 4:40; 13:13).

2) He healed through His word (Matthew 8:8, 16; Luke 4:32, 36; 7:7).

3) At times the Lord rebuked the infirmity or the spirit that caused it (Matthew 17:18; Mark 1:25; 9:25; Luke 4:35, 39; 9:42).

4) People were healed through touching Him or His clothing in faith (Matthew 9:21; 14:36; Mark 3:10; 5:28; 6:56; 8:22; 10:13; Luke 6:19).

5) On a number of occasions Jesus told the seeker, "Thy faith hath made thee whole." (See: Matthew 9:2, 22, 29; 15:28; Mark 2:5; 5:34; 10:52; Luke 5:20; 7:50; 8:48; 18:42.)

6) He placed clay mixed with spittle on the eyes of a blind man (John 9:6-15). This seems to have been a test of simple obedience. The clay had no healing virtue and neither did the spittle. If they did, they would be employed today.

Some wonder about the unbelief in Nazareth hindering the Lord's healing power. They seem to have the idea that unbelief is more powerful than faith, so where there is a great deal of unbelief we cannot expect to have any supernatural power of God. Faith is the most powerful force in the world. Christ said, "If thou canst believe, all things are possible to him that believeth" (Mark 9:23). Doubt cannot conquer faith. It is like light and darkness. You can't bring enough darkness into a room to put out the light! How, then, did unbelief hinder the Lord at Nazareth? Since the people did not believe, they did not give Him a chance to work. He healed all who came to Him, but he did not go around healing people whether they wanted to be healed or not! Unbelief kept the Children of Israel out of the Promised Land (Hebrews 3:19). Unbelief keeps many children of God today from the physical health that the Lord would like them to enjoy. They do not have health because they do not believe the promises and go to the Healer, Jesus Christ.

The earthly ministry of our Lord amply demonstrated his concern for the sick and afflicted. He was "touched with the feeling of our infirmities." What a comfort to know that this ever-present, all-powerful, compassionate Christ is the same yesterday, today, and forever!

He that believeth on me, the works that I do shall he do also.
John 14:12

7

Healing in the Early Church and Through the Centuries

A wonderful thing about the healing ministry of our Lord is that it was not confined to those that He could personally attend. He gave power to His disciples to perform in His name the same type of supernatural healings. First He gave power to the 12 disciples. Matthew 10:1 says: "And when he had called unto him his twelve disciples, he gave them power against unclean spirits, to cast them out, and to heal all manner of sickness and all manner of disease." In verse 8 of the same chapter, He instructed them: "Heal the sick, cleanse the lepers, raise the dead, cast out devils: freely ye have received, freely give." In Luke′s account of this commissioning he says: "Then he called his twelve disciples together, and gave them power and authority over all devils, and to cure diseases. And he sent them to preach the kingdom of God, and to heal the sick" (Luke 9:1, 2). Evidently the Lord intended that the healing ministry should be continued. The Twelve were successful in their assigned work. Verse 6 says: "And they departed, and went through the towns, preaching the gospel, and healing every where."

Many are quick to recognize that the 12 apostles had a healing ministry, but they believe that they were the only ones who were so privileged. After the mission of the Twelve, the Lord chose 70 of His followers and sent them on a similar mission. He told them: "And into whatsoever city ye enter, and they receive you . . . heal the sick that are therein, and say unto them, The kingdom of God is come nigh unto you" (Luke 10:8, 9). What was the result? "And the seventy returned again with joy, saying, Lord, even the devils are subject unto us through thy name" (v. 17). The Lord then gave them that precious promise: "Behold, I give unto you power to tread on serpents and scorpions, and over all the power of the enemy; and nothing shall by any means hurt you" (Luke 10:19). The healing ministry, then, was not limited to the Twelve.

The Great Commission

Still later when the Lord was about to return to heaven, He gave His followers His final orders, the Great Commission. He commanded them: "Go ye into all the world, and preach the gospel to every creature. He that believeth and is baptized shall be saved; but he that believeth not shall be damned. And these signs shall follow them that believe; In my name shall they cast out devils; they shall speak with new tongues; they shall take up serpents; and if they drink any deadly thing, it shall not hurt them; they shall lay hands on the sick, and they shall recover" (Mark 16:15-18).

Notice that the commission was first to the Twelve and then to the Seventy, but now the promise is that these supernatural signs shall follow "them that believe." This is in full agreement with the promise of the Lord: "Verily, verily, I say unto you, He that believeth on me, the works that I do shall he do also; and greater works than these shall he do; because I go unto my Father" (John 14:12). The last clause, "because I go unto my Father," clearly refers to the fact that He would send the Holy Spirit who would enable them to do such feats. In verse 16 He tells them that this Comforter, the Holy Spirit, would abide with them forever.

A further indication that Christ intended that the same type of ministry He had begun would continue is found in John 20:21. Here the resurrected Christ told His followers: "As my Father hath sent me, even so send I you." If the Great Commission is still the responsibility of the Christian, then the supernatural power to carry out the Commission should be the privilege of the Christian also.

(See Acts 1:8.) Remember that Christ had a threefold ministry—to teach, to preach, and to heal. If we are sent as He was, our ministry should follow the same pattern.

Healings in the Early Church

The inspired record shows that these signs did follow the ministry of the early believers. Mark 16:20 tells us that after receiving their orders from the risen Lord, "They went forth, and preached every where, the Lord working with them, and confirming the word with signs following. Amen."

The healing of the lame man at the Gate Beautiful of the temple was the first recorded miracle of healing after Pentecost, when the believers were filled with the Holy Spirit. This was an extraordinary case. The man was lame from birth and was now over 40 years of age. When Peter said, "Such as I have give I thee: In the name of Jesus Christ of Nazareth rise up and walk," the man was instantly healed (Acts 3:1-11). At least 2,000 people believed on Christ as a result of this miracle (Acts 4:4). Peter and John were jailed and commanded not to speak anymore in this name. But they and the other disciples prayed to the Lord to send more healings and wonders (vv. 29, 30). They were then refilled with the Holy Spirit and spoke the Word with boldness.

Soon after this we are told that "by the hands of the apostles were many signs and wonders wrought among the people" (Acts 5:12). Peter seems to have been especially used of the Lord in a ministry of healing. In Acts 5:15, 16 we read: "Insomuch that they brought forth sick into the streets, and laid them on beds and couches, that at the least the shadow of Peter passing by might overshadow some of them. There came also a multitude out of the cities round about unto Jerusalem, bringing sick folks, and them which were vexed with unclean spirits: and they were healed every one." Peter was used of God to heal the paralytic Aeneas (Acts 9:33-35) and to restore to life Dorcas, the lady who has inspired so many Christian women to good works (vv. 36-42).

Stephen, the first martyr, was a man "full of faith and of the Holy Ghost" (Acts 6:5). This is a wonderful combination that is seen all too infrequently. He humbly accepted the job of "waiting tables," i.e., helping in the distribution of food to the widows; however, he did not limit himself to this ministry. In Acts 6:8 we read: "And Stephen, full of faith and power, did great wonders and miracles among the people." He was not of the Twelve or the Seventy, but he was a "believer" and God honored his faith.

Philip, another deacon turned evangelist, went down to Samaria for a campaign. What was the main factor that contributed to his success among those people who were so prejudiced against the Jews? "The people with one accord gave heed unto those things which Philip spake, hearing and seeing the miracles which he did. For unclean spirits, crying with loud voice, came out of many that were possessed with them: and many taken with palsies, and that were lame, were healed. And there was great joy in that city" (Acts 8:6-8).

Paul, the apostle to the Gentiles, was not one of the original Twelve, but he had a remarkable healing ministry. First, he himself was healed of blindness 3 days after his conversion on the Damascus road (Acts 9:18). He was also healed of the bite of a poisonous viper after being shipwrecked on the way to Rome (Acts 28:1-6). On his first missionary journey he and Barnabas encountered strong opposition from a sorcerer called Elymas. This man not only refused the gospel but was doing his utmost to keep a prominent official from believing. Paul was used of God to smite the man with temporary blindness, and the official believed on Christ (Acts 13:6-12).

At Lystra Paul and Barnabas found a man who was crippled from birth. They saw that he had faith to be healed and commanded him to rise up. The man was instantly healed (Acts 14:8-11). Although the people were ready to sacrifice to Paul and Barnabas as gods, a short while later they were turned against them. Paul was then stoned until they thought he was dead and he was dragged out of the city. However, God raised him up and he went on preaching the gospel and encouraging the believers (Acts 14:19-22).

We also have the record of the devil-possessed

fortune-teller who was healed (Acts 16:16-18), as well as the case of Eutychus who was raised from the dead (Acts 20:9, 10). Paul stayed longer in Ephesus than in any other city where he preached. He was there about 3 years (Acts 20:31) and the gospel spread throughout the entire region. The healing ministry seems to have been quite prominent there. In Acts 19:11, 12 we find: "And God wrought special miracles by the hands of Paul: so that from his body were brought unto the sick handkerchiefs or aprons, and the diseases departed from them, and the evil spirits went out of them."

In the closing chapter of the Book of Acts the account of Paul's stay on the island of Malta is given. The father of the chief man of the island, Publius, was sick with a severe case of dysentery. Paul laid hands on him, prayed, and he was healed. After this many of the islanders brought their sick to Paul and they were healed (Acts 28:7-10).

Ministry of Healing Continues

Many have commented on the fact that the Book of Acts does not have an orderly conclusion. It is simply cut off and ends, but one has the feeling that it is not supposed to end, that it should keep right on. I believe that this is significant. The Acts of the Holy Spirit (which some suggest is a more appropriate title for the book) were not intended to stop with the Apostolic Age. The Holy Spirit, the One who gives the power to do these things, was sent to abide with the believers forever. Is it not logical to expect Him to continue doing the same works?

The fact that the gifts of the Spirit were given to the Church to be used for its edification and extension would seem to indicate that these powers would be available as long as they are needed. Among the gifts are those of miracles and healings. The Gentile church in Corinth enjoyed the use and blessing of these gifts. Why should we not have the same privilege?

James wrote to the 12 tribes that were scattered abroad and, in a more general sense, to the entire Church. He gave definite instructions as to what the church should do in the case of an illness of one of its members: "Is any sick among you? let him call for the elders of the church; and let them pray over him, anointing him with oil in the name of the Lord: and the prayer of faith shall save the sick, and the Lord shall raise him up; and if he have committed sins, they shall be forgiven him" (James 5:14, 15). This is the New Testament prescription for the sick believer.

Dr. Gerhard Uhlhorn, in his book *Conflict of Christianity With Heathenism,* says, "Witnesses who are above suspicion leave no room for doubt that the miraculous powers of the apostolic age continued to operate at least into the third century."[1] A. J. Gordon and a number of other writers on the subject quote from several of the Early Church fathers to show that some miraculous healings did occur during the first three centuries of the Christian era. For example: *Justin Martyr* told of demoniacs being delivered and people being healed. *Irenaeus* refers to various gifts and then says, "Others still heal the sick by laying their hands upon them, and they are made whole." *Tertullian* says, "And how many men of rank, to say nothing of the common people, have been delivered from devils and healed of disease." *Origen* refers to people being healed of countless ills, which could be cured by no other means, through faith, and invoking the name of Jesus.

It is generally agreed that a large share of the miraculous powers enjoyed by the Early Church had almost disappeared by the fourth century. This was the era of Constantine, an era of popularity and temporal power for the Church. What the enemy of all righteousness was unable to do under the fierce persecutions the Church went through, he accomplished through popularity and worldliness. It is a known fact that all the water in the world cannot sink a ship as long as it remains outside. When the water gets inside, it can sink the ship. This is true of worldliness and the Church. Fraternizing with the enemy still brings tragic results.

A. J. Gordon says that it is a most suggestive fact that "whenever we find a revival of primitive faith and apostolic simplicity, there we find a profession of the chaste and evangelical miracles which characterized the apostolic age. These attend the cradle of every spiritual reformation, as they did the birth of the Church herself. Waldenses, Moravians, Huguenots, Covenanters, Friends, Baptists and Methodists all have their record of them."[2]

Through the "Dark Ages" of Medieval history many precious truths of the gospel were obscured or lost. Slowly they are being restored to the Church. The Waldensians helped to keep the faith during those trying times. They held among their articles of faith the anointing with oil and prayer for the recovery of the sick. Count Zinzendorf, famous leader of the Moravians, wrote: "To believe against hope is the root of the gift of miracles; and I owe this testimony to our beloved Church, that apostolic powers are there manifested. We have had undeniable proofs thereof in the unequivocal discovery of things, persons and circumstances, which could not humanly have been discovered, in the healing of maladies in themselves incurable, such as cancers, consumptions, when the patient was in the agonies of death, etc., all by means of prayer, or of a single word."[3]

There are recorded instances of healing in answer to prayer under the ministry of Martin Luther, John Wesley, John Welch, George Fox, and J. N. Darby. Many of God's choice servants have themselves experienced healing that was undeniably supernatural and divine. For example, we can cite Andrew Murray, A. B. Simpson, Samuel Chadwick, and E. Stanley Jones. We do not have the space to give the details of these healings but the examples can be multiplied. A. J. Gordon, of Boston; Andrew Murray, of South Africa; and A. B. Simpson, of New York; were among the first in the 19th century to make a thorough study of the subject of divine healing, accept it as a doctrine, and write on the subject. Their writings are worthy of careful consideration.

In view of the foregoing, we can say that there is sufficient evidence that divine healing did not stop with the Apostolic Age but has continued even up to the 20th century.

Once more I would like to quote from the writing of A. J. Gordon: "If we find there is no abrupt termination of miracles with the expiration of the Apostolic Age, then we must begin to raise the question why should there be any termination at all, so long as the Church remains, and the ministry of the Spirit is perpetuated?"[4] Indeed, why should healings cease at all? We have the same needs and we have the same Physician who is able to meet all those needs. "These signs *shall follow* them that believe" (Mark 16:17).

8

Healing in the 20th Century

One of the attributes of deity is immutability. God never changes. Just as the fixed orbit God has set for the planets is dependable, so is the God who orders their courses unchanging. Why are we always seeking change? It is because we have not reached perfection. Any deviation from perfection would necessarily be toward imperfection. Since God is perfect, He must not, He cannot change. Anything He was able to do in the past He is able to do now. Anything He was willing to do in the past He is willing to do now. If God healed in Old Testament times, if He healed in the days of Christ, if He healed in apostolic and post-apostolic days, then why should we not expect Him to heal in the 20th century or any other century until He returns?

Our sources of information are admittedly scarce when it comes to many of the centuries of medieval times. However, when we come to the 20th century the sources are so abundant that it is difficult to select the information that is most pertinent to our discussion.

A number of men and women who have been used of God in a healing ministry will be mentioned in this chapter. Most, if not all, of these would reject the term *faith healer*. They did not possess any mystical powers of their own. They insisted that people should "look to Jesus" for their healing. Any benefit offered was in the name and through the power of Jesus Christ. Some of the people mentioned have been fiercely opposed. People don't like to change their religious views, and some strongly resent

60

the intrusion of any new doctrine that would upset their cherished traditions. Although we may have our doctrinal differences, we must admit that God has used these servants of His. Remember, too, that the devil, "the accuser of the brethren," opposes most those who do the greatest harm to his cause.

During the 19th century the interest in the subject of divine healing began to increase. Some homes were established for those who sought healing through faith in Jesus Christ. One of the most notable of these was that of Dorothea Trudel (1813-1862) in the Swiss village of Mannendorf on Lake Zurich. Many cases of miraculous healing were recorded as a result of this "house of prayer." Pastor John C. Blumhardt (1805-1880) had a similar ministry in the small Lutheran village of Mottlingen in the heart of the Black Forest in Germany. Pastor Blumhardt, after graduating from the University of Tubingen, saw a woman delivered from what seemed to be demon possession in answer to his prayers. The entire village was stirred. He sought and received "power from on high," and God used him greatly in praying for the sick. He moved to larger quarters at Bad Boll where the government sold him a building at less than cost, and the king made a special donation to help him start his work. There the sick went for healing from all over Europe and even from America.[1] His prayers of faith were greatly honored of God. In the United States, a Dr. Charles Cullis (1833-1892) had a faith work in the city of Boston where many found the Lord to be their Healer.

There were several well-known ministers whose writings helped prepare the way for the wide dissemination of the gospel of healing. Some believe that Otto Stockmayer deserves the title of "The Theologian of the Doctrine of Healing by Faith." He published his views on the subject and later established a home in Switzerland where many were healed.[2] Some outstanding ministers who wrote and published serious works on divine healing were:

Andrew Murray (1828-1917), a deeply respected minister of the Dutch Reformed Church of South Africa; A. J. Gordon (1836-1895), a Baptist pastor of Boston; R. A.

Torrey (1856-1928), evangelist, writer, and first president of Moody Bible Institute; and A. B. Simpson, founder of the Christian and Missionary Alliance.

Healing Ministries in the 20th Century

A. B. Simpson experienced a most remarkable healing after suffering nervous collapses, a severe heart condition, and many other physical ailments for over 20 years. He received health and strength enough to climb mountains. For years he continued with a most strenuous schedule involving a tremendous output of labor, but suffered little fatigue and no exhaustion. His personal testimony is inspiring.[3]

One of the first evangelists to hold large campaigns and pray for the sick in the U.S.A. was Mary B. Woodworth-Etter, whose public ministry began about 1877. This unusual woman held meetings all over the country. Thousands testified that they had received physical healing in answer to her prayers.

Alexander Dowie began his ministry as a Congregational pastor in Australia. He soon began to believe the doctrine of divine healing. During campaigns his healing ministry drew crowds of up to 20,000. In 1888 he moved to America where he eventually founded the city of Zion, Illinois. It is said of him, "Dr. Dowie did more to promote the doctrine of divine healing than possibly any other man. He was arrested 100 times for praying for the sick. Thousands were saved and healed under his ministry."[4] Dowie held doctrines that were unacceptable to most evangelical churches, and this is doubtlessly one reason his ministry has been so little publicized.

Charles Parham (1873-1929) was one of the first leaders of the Pentecostal movement. Parham's doctrine, however, did not begin to spread until some miraculous healings began to accompany his ministry. Pentecostal groups throughout the world hold many different doctrinal beliefs, but are all united on the fundamental truths of salvation, divine healing, the baptism in the Holy Spirit, and the second coming of Christ.

Aimee Semple McPherson (1890-1944) began her evangelistic work in Canada in 1910. Healings of almost every imaginable disease took place in her campaigns. The crowds thronged the largest auditoriums available in principal cities across Canada and the United States. She was the founder of the International Church of the Foursquare Gospel.

Dr. Charles S. Price was a Congregational pastor in California. He was popular as a chautauqua lecturer. He was disturbed by the reports of Aimee McPherson's meetings and decided he would expose the fraud. He attended one of her meetings and was completely convinced by the evidence of God's power at work. He was a changed man and devoted the remainder of his life to evangelistic work. Great crowds and miracles of healing characterized his meetings in the United States and Canada.

Lorne Fox was a hopeless cripple when Dr. Price came to the Canadian city where he lived. God miraculously healed him, and he has been preaching the gospel for years with similar results. He has held successful campaigns on many mission fields.

P. C. Nelson (1868-1942) was the pastor of a Baptist church in Detroit, Michigan. He was struck by an automobile when he was getting off a streetcar, suffering a very serious and painful knee injury that even threatened his life. An infection got into the synovial sacs around the knee and the doctor told him he could expect to be lame for many months. If his life could be saved, he should not be surprised if his knee would become permanently stiff. In answer to the prayer of faith he was instantly healed. He too became an evangelist with supernatural healings taking place in his campaigns. However, he later gave up this ministry to establish a Bible college where workers could be trained to perpetuate this same ministry. The motto of the college was: "The Whole Gospel, for the Whole World."

F. F. Bosworth was one of the early preachers of the gospel of healing. He expounded the Word of God on the subject with great clarity and with good results.

Raymond T. Richie was well known for his great faith. He did not attempt to approach the eloquence of other prominent evangelists, but his humble sincerity and simple faith brought salvation and healing to thousands of people. He held many large and remarkable campaigns across the country.

Francisco Olazabel was used of the Lord to take the gospel with "signs following" to many thousands of Spanish-speaking people in New York and on the Mexican border.

Great Britain also had some evangelists that reached vast multitudes with the full gospel message. Outstanding among these was Smith Wigglesworth (1859-1947). Wigglesworth was a dedicated youth in the Salvation Army. He had little formal education. His life was transformed by a charismatic experience he received in Sunderland. One of his biographers calls him an "apostle of faith." There were so many healing miracles wherever he preached that his services were in great demand. He held campaigns in Great Britain, Australia, New Zealand, Canada, and many countries of Europe. He also held frequent meetings in the U.S.

Stephen Jeffreys (1867-1943) and his brother George had an extraordinary ministry in Great Britain. The miracles of healing which followed their ministry attracted a great deal of attention. Newspapers gave publicity to the campaigns. Some reports were favorable and some were not. Their meetings filled large auditoriums such as the Royal Albert Hall in London. They established the Elim Churches of England; churches known for their evangelistic zeal.

For a time it seemed there was little emphasis on the doctrine of divine healing in evangelical circles. In the late 1940's a number of evangelists began proclaiming the doctrine anew. It is true that there were some who capitalized on the universal longing for health and over-advertized and commercialized the message, thus bringing the doctrine into disrepute. At the same time there was a genuine move of God which brought faith, hope, and healing to multiplied thousands around the world. We must not discredit a Biblical doctrine simply because some misinterpret, distort, misapply, or attempt to use it as a means of personal aggrandizement.

There are a number of well-known evangelists in our day who have brought the message of salvation and healing to multitudes around the world. Campaigns held by these evangelists have sometimes stirred entire nations and opened many doors to the preaching of the gospel.

There is no way of estimating the number of healings that could be classified as miraculous which have taken place in the meetings of these evangelists. Many of those healed have clinical case histories with X rays, doctors' statements, and other documentation to prove their testimonies.

It would be impossible to give more than a mere fraction of the healings I know of personally. On the four continents and several islands where I have worked I have seen supernatural healings in answer to prayer both in my own ministry and in that of others with whom I have been closely associated. To me, the veracity of these healings is not a matter of theory, conjecture, or speculation—it is a proven reality.

In declaring the gospel of Jesus Christ to King Agrippa, Paul said: "This thing was not done in a corner" (Acts 26:26). One may not understand the doctrine and may never have personally seen anything that could be called a miracle, but there is enough published evidence so that anyone who desires to can examine the facts and be assured that God does heal in the 20th century. For example, the *Pentecostal Evangel,* the official weekly publication of the Assemblies of God, has for years published the testimonies of different people who have been supernaturally healed in answer to prayer. These testimonies must always be verified and endorsed by a pastor before publication is allowed. There may be a waiting period of some months and then a further verification. Every precaution is taken to assure the publication of only *bona fide* testimonies that will stand up to any investigation, and yet there is no shortage of testimonies of God's healing today! A careful reading of the testimonies in some of the books listed in the bibliography will be a real inspiration and blessing.

Another type of healing that should be mentioned is deliverance from drug addiction. Drug abuse has become one of the major problems of our world today. First, because of its devastating effects on the body and mind of those who become addicted, and second, because of the crimes committed to get money for a habit that may cost $100 or more per day. Medical cures are, according to available statistics, ineffective in over 90 percent of the cases treated. However, hundreds if not thousands of addicts are finding a complete cure in Jesus Christ. The Teen Challenge centers in most of our major cities in the U.S. are being recognized as one of the most effective measures yet discovered for the permanent cure of drug addicts. The entire emphasis of Teen Challenge is Jesus Christ. After a complete surrender of his life to Jesus the patient is surrounded by prayer, and through the aid of the Holy Spirit is enabled to kick the habit completely, many times without any withdrawal pains. Medical doctors and government officials that are familiar with the problems of drug abuse are amazed at the results. These Teen Challenge centers are now being established in many parts of Europe. The same results are being seen there also.

The maximum number of witnesses required by law is said to be 7. This is for the establishment of an oral will. The writer of the Epistle to the Hebrews mentions a "great . . . cloud of witnesses" (Hebrews 12:1). The number of witnesses is certainly sufficient to establish the fact that "Jesus Christ [is] the same yesterday, and today, and for ever" (Hebrews 13:8). He still has compassion; He still has power; He still saves; *and He still heals*.

. . . to another the gifts of healings . . . to another the working of miracles. 1 Corinthians 12:9, 10

9

Gifts of Healings and Working of Miracles

A study of the doctrine of divine healing would not be complete without a careful look at the gifts of the Holy Spirit, especially the gifts of healings and of miracles. Paul wrote to the church in Corinth: "Now concerning spiritual gifts, brethren, I would not have you ignorant" (1 Corinthians 12:1). Unfortunately, a great many of God's children today seem to be very uninformed when it comes to spiritual gifts. E. S. Williams, referring to the purpose of spiritual gifts, says, "They are spiritual enablements for the purpose of building up the Church of God. They are also given as signs for the confirmation of the Truth to the World."[1]

Mistaken Ideas About the Gifts

Some have been led to believe that the gifts of the Spirit are not for us today. They quote from 1 Corinthians 13:8 and say that "tongues shall cease." However, the same verse says that knowledge will "vanish away." Has this happened yet? A careful reading of the context makes it very clear that these imperfect operations will cease when that which is perfect comes. This will be at the coming of Christ. The gifts were given by Christ to His church—spiritual enablements for a spiritual warfare— and we would be foolish to ignore them or go to battle without them.

Many have a mistaken idea about the nature of these gifts. There are some who believe that God gives a person one or more of these gifts and they become his exclusive property to do with as he pleases. They believe that he can call them into operation at any time he desires. First, let us note that in 1 Corinthians 12:1 the word *gifts* is in italics. This means that it has been supplied by the translators and is not in the original text. A more literal rendering would be: "Concerning spirituals, brethren, I would not have you ignorant." Going down to verse 7, "But the manifestation of the Spirit is given to every man to profit withal" (KJV), or "for tne common good" (Moffatt).

A word from R. E. McAlister will be helpful here: "We further note that the word *gifts* in 1 Corinthians 12:4, is translated from the Greek word *charisma*. Greek scholars give at least five shades of meaning to this Greek word, as follows: grace, favor, kindness, gift and help."[2] All this seems to indicate that the Lord has conceded this grace to His church that the work of the Holy Spirit might be manifested. If we can get away from the idea of certain divine powers being bestowed upon a select few while the majority of the members sit by without participating, and realize that the Holy Spirit may manifest himself through any of the members of the body of Christ at any time, we will make real spiritual progress. Remember that we are not made vast reservoirs of the mighty power of God, but are channels through which the Holy Spirit can flow and do His work. He is the Source of power. We are but the earthen vessels He uses. Speaking on this subject Dennis Bennett says: "This mistake—claiming to have permanent gifts—leads to pride, to stagnation, and tends to limit God's other gifts in that person. Another result is a focusing down on a few people to express the gifts while the majority of the congregation sits by as spectators with no expectation that God may want to work through them."[3]

Some throw out a challenge today and say, "Where are the gifts of healing?" They say that if any possess such powers they should go to the hospitals and heal everyone there. There is no Biblical precedent for this sort of thing. Jesus healed all who came to Him for healing, but He did not heal indiscriminately. There were many sufferers by the pool of Bethesda, but Christ chose to heal only one. Would you say that He did not have the gift?

Gifts Are Manifestations of the Spirit

It is well to remember that all the gifts of the Spirit operate in the realm of the supernatural. They have nothing to do with medical knowledge or skill but are divine interventions for the relief and cure of physical ailments. When Paul and his company landed on the island of Malta and found a leading citizen very sick with dysentery, it was not Luke the physician that prescribed medicine for him, but Paul who prayed for him—and he was completely healed (Acts 28:1-10).

There are three gifts of the Spirit that are associated with physical healing. They are the gifts of healings, the gift of miracles, and the gift of faith. Faith will be discussed in a later chapter, but we will study the other two at this time.

We have already seen that the different gifts of the Spirit are in reality manifestations of the Holy Spirit and His work. It seems that the description of the operation of these ministries of the Spirit given in 1 Corinthians 12 is that of a meeting in a local assembly. The Spirit manifests himself through first one person and then another in various ways. He gives to one a word of wisdom, to another a prophecy, to another a message in tongues, and so on. Verse 11 tells us, "But all these worketh that one and the selfsame Spirit, dividing to every man severally as he will."

When God uses a person repeatedly for the manifestation of one of the gifts it is said that he has a ministry along that line. Since "gifts of healings" and "miracles" are listed in verse 28 among the ministries God has set in the Church along with apostles, prophets, and teachers, it can be concluded that certain people have been given a ministry of bringing healing to the sick through the power of the Holy Spirit. The individual, therefore, does not need to say that he has a special "gift," (which is so often misinterpreted), but that he has a "ministry." I have known evangelists and pastors that had remarkable results in praying for the sick and still did not claim any special "gift." In fact, there are those who say the person healed is the one who receives the "gift," and not the person who prays for him.

Although we often speak of the "gift of healing," in the Greek both words are in the plural. There seems to be nothing that specifically indicates why the plural is used here. Since there are so many different kinds of diseases and infirmities, some believe that different healing powers may be referred to here. Also, it is quite possible that some would have more faith to pray for some types of infirmities than other kinds. It is suggested that in dealing with evil spirits for the liberation of their victims, a special enduement of power might be needed. If we take the position that the "gifts of healings" are the healings themselves which the thousands of sick receive, then it would be natural to use the plural with reference to these manifestations of the Holy Spirit.

What About Miracles?

It has often been declared from the pulpit that the day of miracles is past. On what authority do men make such a statement? Can we have healings today, but nothing of a miraculous nature? Are all healings miracles?

First, let us establish a definition of *miracle*. One definition is as follows: "An event that appears to be neither a part nor result of any known natural law or agency, and is therefore often attributed to a supernatural or divine source."[4] A root meaning of the word is "something that causes wonder or astonishment." There are those who try to reject everything miraculous on the grounds that God has established certain laws in nature and He will not break or annul those laws. We agree with the theologian Berkhof when he says: "When a miracle is performed, the laws of nature are not violated, but superseded at a particular point by a higher manifestation of the will of God. The forces of nature are not annihilated or suspended, but are only counteracted at a particular point by a force superior to the powers of nature."[5]

Speaking of miracles, Harold Horton says: "A miracle is a supernatural intervention in the ordinary course of nature; a temporary suspension of the accustomed order; an interruption of the system of nature as we know it. . . . A miracle is a sovereign act of the Spirit of God irrespective of the laws or systems. . . . God is not bound by His own laws. . . . To speak of God as though He were circumscribed by the laws of His own making is to reduce to the creature plane and impair the very essence of His eternal attributes."[6]

Here is a simple illustration. The law of gravity attracts to the earth all objects heavier than the air. When a giant plane takes off and rises into the sky carrying many tons of cargo, the law of gravity has not been suspended or annulled. The power of the mighty jet engines has overcome the pull of gravity. God is able to take over at any time and do that which to us would be miraculous.

There are miracles of many different kinds recorded in the Bible. There were the nonhealing types of miracles, such as the parting of the Red Sea and the Jordan, the descent of fire from heaven to consume the sacrifice on the altar at Mt. Carmel, the provision of water from the rock and manna from heaven. There were also many healing miracles performed by the Lord and by His followers. The healing of the lame man at the Gate Beautiful of the temple was called a miracle (Acts 4:16). The raising of Lazarus after 3 days in the tomb was certainly a miracle. Many others could be cited.

Contrary to what some believe and teach, miracles did not stop with Christ and His apostles. A. J. Gordon says that Professor Pfleiderer calls the dictum that miracles ceased with the Apostolic Age, "an extraordinary assumption of Protestant dogmatism" and a "postulate which both history and experience entirely contradict."[7] God has not changed; He can still perform miracles whenever He pleases.

Many healings seem to be miraculous. What is the difference, if any, between the gifts of healing and the gift of miracles? We have already noted that some miracles have nothing to do with physical healing. There are those that believe miracles must be instantaneous while healing (even divine healing) might take time for its completion. I'm not sure that this distinction can be made. Hudson Taylor, the great man of faith who founded the China Inland Mission, said that a miracle usually has three stages: first, impossible; second, difficult; and third, done. It would seem that there is a certain blending of some of the manifestations of the Spirit so that there are no sharply defined lines between them in their operation. This is especially true in the gifts of power: faith, healing, and miracles.

What is the purpose of miracles? Although we freely admit that God can perform as many miracles as He chooses as often as He pleases, both Biblical and Church history seems to indicate that God uses miracles sparingly. Herod wanted Christ to perform some miracle for his entertainment. The Lord would not consent to any such thing (Luke 23:8-11). Jesus rebuked those who wanted to see a sign (Matthew 16:1-4). Speaking on this subject, C.M. Ward says: "The ministry of Jesus was gifted with miracles. A careful study of when He did employ a miracle and when He did not employ a miracle will lead to these conclusions: (1) He did not provide by a miracle what could be provided by human endeavor or human foresight. (2) He would not use His special powers to provide for His personal wants. (3) He would not work a miracle merely for a miracle's sake. It was always associated with benevolence and instruction. (4) He would not supplement policy or human directive by a miracle. (5) He worked no miracle that became overwhelming in awfulness so as to terrify men into acceptance, or which would be unanswerably certain, leaving men no loophole for unbelief."[8]

There are three different Greek words that are used in the New Testament for "miracles."

(1) *teras*—meaning a prodigy, omen, or wonder.

(2) *dunamis*—signifying miraculous power.

(3) *semeion*—a miracle, token, sign, or wonder.

Besides being translated "miracle," these words are sometimes translated "wonder," "mighty works," "signs," and so on.

John the apostle consistently used the word *semeion* to describe the works of Christ. This usage emphasizes the "sign" value of the miracles. A sign is not important in itself, but for what it points out or indicates. Thus the miracles of Christ were important for what they pointed to.

John selected only seven miracles from a far greater number and wrote these down with a definite purpose in view. He clearly stated his purpose in these terms: "And many other signs truly did Jesus in the presence of his disciples, which are not written in this book: but these are written, that ye might believe that Jesus is the Christ, the Son of God; and that believing ye might have life through his name" (John 20:30, 31). A main purpose of a miracle, then, is to cause people to believe that Jesus Christ is the Son of God, the Saviour of the world, so that believing they may have eternal life through Him.

A well-known Pharisee and ruler of the Jews told Jesus, "We know that thou art a teacher come from God: for no man can do these miracles that thou doest, except God be with him" (John 3:2). On the Day of Pentecost, Peter in his sermon to the assembled multitude referred to Christ as "Jesus of Nazareth, a man approved of God among you by miracles and wonders and signs, which God did by him in the midst of you, as ye yourselves also know" (Acts 2:22).

Jesus cited His miraculous works as an evidence of His messiahship to the messengers of John the Baptist (Matthew 11:2-5). John the Baptist was recognized by Christ as one of the greatest men ever born. He proclaimed that Jesus was the Son of God (John 1:34). However, Jesus said that the works He did were greater evidence of His divine origin than the witness of John (John 5:36). In fact, Jesus went as far as to say that it would not be a sin to disbelieve Him if He had not done mighty works (miracles) before them (John 15:24).

The Lord's disciples were given the Great Commission to take the gospel to all the world. They were told that miraculous signs would follow those who believe. They believed and obeyed. The result? "They went forth, and preached every where, the Lord working with them, and confirming the word with signs following. Amen" (Mark 16:20). In the Epistle to the Hebrews we are told that the Lord began to announce the great plan of salvation, and then it was confirmed by those who had heard Him: "God also bearing them witness, both with signs and wonders, and with divers miracles, and gifts of the Holy Ghost" (Hebrews 2:4).

We believe that the Great Commission is still binding upon Christians today. If the command is still in force, the power to effect the order must still be available. The Holy Spirit was sent to abide with us forever. Surely His gifts of power will always be given to those who sincerely trust Him for these divine enablements. The gifts of the Spirit are most desirable for an effective ministry to the sick.

Miracles Needed Today

The supernatural power of God manifested in the miraculous healing of the sick is greatly needed in today's skeptical world. There are many "Nicodemuses" now that need to be convinced by such demonstrations of the power of the living God. However, a word of caution is in order for those who would seek to be used of God in this manner. We should be careful to avoid the "magical" in our search for the "miraculous." God performs many miracles that are not "spectacular." We should always have in mind that the test of a true miracle of God is, "What good does it accomplish?" A miracle (semeion) should always point to the miracle worker, Jesus Christ, and not to the one who is simply an instrument in God's hands.

The fact that there are so many millions of sufferers all around us who need to experience the healing that only Christ can give is a great motivation for seeking the gifts of healings and of miracles. Nevertheless, it is very easy for our hearts to deceive us into thinking that our motives are pure when there is a large percentage of self-seeking in our inner thoughts. We long for the publicity, the fame, the crowds, and perhaps even the financial reward such a ministry could conceivably bring. An orator may attract hundreds, while a "miracle worker" would attract thousands. It is hard to keep the victory over success. Crowd-intoxication can result in serious spiritual damage. We must be sure that we have the right motives— compassion for the sick in body and soul and a sincere desire to see that our wonderful Lord receives all the glory which He so richly deserves.

10

Christians Should Be Healthy

Christians who have been "born again" and are filled with the Holy Spirit should be the healthiest people in the world! Let me tell you why.

Not long ago I read a newspaper article titled "Adventist Males Just Live Longer." This was the conclusion reached after a careful survey had been made comparing Seventh-Day Adventists with the national norm for longevity. Though they are noted for their temperate life-style, Seventh-Day Adventists are not the only Christians who enjoy better than average health. Consider with me the following four reasons why Christians should be healthy: (1) Temperate lives; (2) Emotional balance; (3) Divine protection; and (4) The life of Christ within.

Temperate Lives

A Christian should be healthy because he does not indulge in many things that are harmful to physical health. Dr. Karl Menninger states that on March 19, 1972 the evil of self-administered drugs was officially called "America's No. 1 Problem."[1] It is difficult for most of us to realize the extent of this problem. Besides the thousands who are in our mental institutions because drugs have literally "blown their minds," there are those who die because of overdoses or from experimenting with little-known drugs. There are thousands of young people who are wasting away physically, while their only desire seems to be just another "fix." Put this together with the tremendous upsurge of crimes committed to secure money to buy drugs, and you can easily see why this can be called a number one problem. (The percentage increase of this type of crime in the U.S. from 1967 to 1972 is reported to be as follows: robbery 85.5 percent; burglary 45.6 percent; larceny 75.1 percent.)[2]

We know that a good Christian does not abuse his body by taking L.S.D., "speed," and other similar drugs; but perhaps some need to be warned against the milder forms of drug usage—pills to stay awake, pills to go to sleep, pills to calm nerves, etc. The fact that many people have died from an overdose of sleeping pills should alert us to the dangers of such drugs.

Although the use of the more notorious drugs may be considered the number one problem, Dr. Menninger says that *alcohol and nicotine* harm far more people. We are aware of the disastrous effects of drunken drivers on our streets and highways. They caused the death of more than 25,000 people last year. Statistics from one survey show that alcohol was a factor in over 40 percent of the violent deaths in our country. Alcohol is also a factor in many suicides. Many seem to ignore the fact that some 10 percent of the admissions to our overcrowded mental institutions are officially reported as due to alcoholism, and in the case of an additional 10 percent alcoholism is listed as an important contributing cause. It is reported that about 6 percent of chronic alcoholics develop insanity in some form.[3] When we consider the total number of alcoholics in our country and the rate at which this is increasing, we can begin to understand something of the magnitude of this problem.

Hardening of the liver, partial paralysis of certain muscles, neuritis, inflammation of the lining of the stomach, gastric cancer, and a weakening of resistance to other diseases are some of the physical consequences of alcoholic indulgence. The Bible strongly condemns drunkenness. If you don't take the first drink, you will never become a drunkard. A dedicated Christian who consistently refuses even a social drink can normally expect better health and longer life than those whose bodies continually have to fight off the poisons of alcohol.

On a national broadcast of the ABC television network

on July 20, 1974, the news commentator Harry Reasoner stated: "Ten years after the surgeon general's warning, there are 50 million Americans who still smoke." One doctor after carefully examining the facts states:

If one were to total the deaths from cancer of the lung and other areas of the body, plus the deaths from apoplexy, pneumonia, influenza, tuberculosis, emphysema, asthma, ulcers and coronary heart trouble—deaths in which tobacco plays a major role—the grand total would be between two hundred thousand and three hundred thousand Americans per year.[4]

Of the 50 million Americans who smoke, there are many millions who would like to quit but seem unable to do so. The Christian realizes his body is a temple of the Holy Spirit and wants to keep that temple serviceable and clean. He not only has the will to stop smoking, drinking, and habitually using drugs, but the power of the Spirit of God has enabled him to do so. His health should then be much better than that of those who are dependent on drugs, alcohol, and tobacco.

Venereal diseases are a major problem in the U.S. and many parts of the world. For a while they seemed to be on the decrease, but then they began to skyrocket. In a recent 4-year period, reported cases of syphilis increased by 200 to 800 percent in several major cities. The main cause of this increase seems to be the decline of moral standards. Since the Bible is very explicit in its denunciation of all manner of illicit sex, the Christian who lives by its standard does not have to fear the dread results of these terrible diseases. He is a healthier person because he scrupulously avoids the causes of the so-called "social diseases."

Gluttony is not so easy to discuss, because it comes closer to home than some of the more open vices. The problem of obesity and its effects on health has already been mentioned. The apostle Paul tells us that an athlete who really wants to win is temperate in all things. This, he tells us, is only to win a crown that will soon pass away. How much more should we who are striving for an eternal reward make every effort to bring under control anything that would hinder us from being at our very best for the

Lord! (1 Corinthians 9:25). Proper diet and eating habits are very important for anyone who wants to be at his best physically. And anyone who works at a sedentary occupation must be sure to get sufficient physical exercise. If we know to do good and don't do it, that is sin! (See James 4:17.) Paul gives a good rule to go by: "Whether therefore ye eat, or drink, or whatsoever ye do, do all to the glory of God" (1 Corinthians 10:31).

Emotional Balance

The public at large does not recognize how many illnesses have their origin in emotional imbalance. For example, we are told that some 7 million Americans are treated everyday for some type of back ailment. Dr. John Sarno of the Institute of Rehabilitation Medicine in New York believes that emotions, tensions, anxiety, and depression are a significant factor in at least 80 percent of back troubles.[5] In the preface of his very helpful and well-documented book *None of These Diseases*, Dr. S. I. McMillen states:

> Medical science recognizes that emotions such as fear, sorrow, envy, resentment, and hatred are responsible for the majority of our sicknesses. Estimates vary from 60 percent to nearly 100 percent.
> Emotional stress can cause high blood pressure, toxic goiter, migraine headaches, arthritis, apoplexy, heart trouble, gastro-intestinal ulcers, and other serious diseases too numerous to mention. As physicians we can prescribe medicine for the symptoms of these diseases, but we cannot do much for the underlying cause—emotional turmoil.[6]

This is where Christianity comes in. God can completely change a man and help him overcome all his harmful emotions. It is easy to see how such a transformation would greatly contribute to the well-being of the true Christian. Let us now examine some specific emotions that can cause damage to health and learn how to deal with them. Anger is high on the list of damaging emotions. Hatred, resentment and bitterness are all condemned in the Word of God. What is the antidote? Love. We love God. We love our families. We love our brothers and sisters in Christ. This love is good and is commanded by our Lord. In fact, our love for one another is a badge of discipleship. "By this shall all men know that ye are my disciples, if ye have love one to another" (John 13:35). However, our love should not stop there. We are told to love even our enemies. Christ exemplified this type of love when He prayed for those who were crucifying Him. We are to be so filled with the love of God that it will be impossible for us to hate anyone. This will have a healthy effect on our lives!

Fear, worry, and a sense of insecurity build up tensions that are most harmful to our physical well-being. A Christian can have victory over all these. Over and over again the Word of God tells us "Fear not!" Even in the presence of death, Jesus told a distraught parent: "Be not afraid, only believe" (Mark 5:36). The One who said, "All power is given unto me in heaven and in earth," has also promised, "Lo, I am with you alway, even unto the end of the world" (Matthew 28:18, 20). He not only has all power and is continually with us, but He is concerned with our welfare. He cares. His Word tells us we can cast our care upon Him because He cares for us. (See 1 Peter 5:7.) The safest place in the world is the center of the will of God. The Psalmist declares: "God is our refuge and strength, a very present help in trouble. Therefore will not we fear, though the earth be removed, and though the mountains be carried into the midst of the sea" (Psalm 46:1, 2). Let us say with David: "The Lord is my light and my salvation; whom shall I fear? The Lord is the strength of my life; of whom shall I be afraid?" (Psalm 27:1). Remember that "there is no fear in love; but perfect love casteth out fear" (1 John 4:18). Secure in God's protecting hand, free from fear and worry, the trusting Christian should enjoy the blessing of good health.

Psychologists and psychiatrists agree that it is very important to the small child to know that someone really loves him. If he feels rejected or unwanted, it can cause serious problems to his health and to his personality. Older folks also need to know that someone cares for them. One wealthy man who lived alone said, "I would give anything if there was just someone who cared whether I came home late from work." Loneliness, a sense of rejection, or a feeling that no one cares, can lead to dejection, despondency, and in many cases to ill health or even suicide. Thank God, Christians can always know that they have "a friend that sticketh closer than a brother" (Proverbs 18:24). He loves us sincerely, as His sacrifice demonstrates. God loves us because it is His nature to love, just as a rose gives out its perfume because it is a rose. Since His love does not depend on the "lovableness" of the person loved, it is neither spasmodic nor transient, but constant and eternal. The Lord says, "Yea, I have loved thee with an everlasting love: therefore with loving-kindness have I drawn thee" (Jeremiah 31:3). If we know that God really loves us, we will be free from the fear and insecurity many people suffer today.

A very wise man said, "A merry heart doeth good like a medicine: but a broken spirit drieth the bones" (Proverbs 17:22). Happiness is very important to our health and general well-being, and yet how few people appear to be really happy! How many smiling faces do you see on the busy streets of our cities? Genuine joy is a fruit of the Spirit, as listed in Galatians 5:22. Romans 14:17 speaks of "joy in the Holy Ghost." Paul writes the church in Philippi and exhorts them saying: "Rejoice in the Lord always: and again I say, Rejoice" (Philippians 4:4). We may not always be able to rejoice in circumstances, but we can always rejoice in the Lord. A great leader and governor of the Jewish people, just returned from Babylonian exile, told his people not to be sad but to rejoice, for "the joy of the Lord is your strength" (Nehemiah 8:10). It is hard for the devil to tempt a really happy Christian. What can allure a truly satisfied person? Joy is a very healthy emotion.

Mental health is believed by some doctors to embrace the physical, social, cultural, spiritual, and all other realms of health. It is most important that the communications center which directs all the activities of the body be kept in good condition. The Christian has a promise that "the peace of God, which passeth all understanding, shall keep your hearts and minds through Christ Jesus" (Philippians 4:7). Of course there are conditions to be met, but they are reasonable. First, we need to have peace *with* God, and then we can have the peace *of* God. Christ's parting gift to His followers was peace. He said, "Peace I leave with you, my peace I give unto you: not as the world giveth, give I unto you. Let not your heart be troubled, neither let it be afraid" (John 14:27). Thought control is perhaps the most difficult task that faces the Christian. Since thoughts produce actions, we must make the necessary effort to rule our thoughts and not indulge in harmful thinking. It is well to remember that you cannot exclude thoughts from your mind by simply saying to yourself, "I'm not going to think about - - - - - -." You have to fill your mind with other thoughts. In view of this, the apostle Paul gives us in Philippians 4:8 a list of things to think on. A somewhat paraphrased version of the main thoughts is found in the following verse:

Whatsoever things are lovely, Whatsoever things are true, Whatsoever things are honest, Those things would I think and do.
May I seek in others virtue, Never blame but always praise.
To the good report I'd listen, Heart and hands in prayer e'er raise.
Just and pure in all my dealings, and in all my thoughts I'd be,
For God's Word has plainly told us,
    "As one thinketh, so is he."

                                        H.P.J.

When asked for the secret of his life of spiritual victory and blessing, one eminent Christian leader said that he made Christ the home of his thoughts. We often have to go to work or school and leave home temporarily, but when we are free we automatically turn toward home. Whenever our mind is free from necessary tasks it should return to its home—Christ.

Divine Protection

The Christian should be healthy not only because he is temperate and has good emotional balance but because he has protection that others do not have. There is a difference between those who are the Lord's children and those who are not. When God delivered the Israelites from their bondage He sent plagues on their oppressors—not on His people. The Israelites had light while the others were in darkness. The Lord promised that He would not send the diseases upon them that had come upon others (Exodus 15:26).

The 91st Psalm is a most comforting and reassuring song of protection. In it we are told that we will have no need to fear the evil that comes upon those around us while we are under the shelter of the wings of the Almighty. Verse 10 says: "There shall no evil befall thee, neither shall any plague come nigh thy dwelling." In the 34th Psalm we are told, "The angel of the Lord encampeth round about them that fear him, and delivereth them" (v 7).

This is health and accident insurance of the best kind—protection against sickness and accidents rather than financial help when such things occur. In Ezekiel 34 we are told that a good shepherd heals his sheep. This is a part of his responsibility—to search out those that are lame, wounded, weak, or sick and help them back to health. Christ is the Good Shepherd. He dearly loves the sheep that He bought with the price of His own blood. He will protect, defend, and provide for all the needs of His flock. We have nothing to fear as we follow our Good Shepherd.

The Life of Christ Within

One of the greatest mysteries of the Christian faith is that of the indwelling Christ. Although it is very difficult to understand how God would condescend to dwell in such unworthy mortals as we, it is plainly taught in the Scriptures. Jesus said, "If a man love me, he will keep my words: and my Father will love him, and we will come unto him, and make our abode with him" (John 14:23). He will actually live within us! In fact, Paul says that Christ in us is the hope of glory (Colossians 1:27). The apostle John says, "God hath given to us eternal life, and this life is in his Son. He that hath the Son hath life; and he that hath not the Son of God hath not life" (1 John 5:11, 12).

We all recognize that Christ came to bring spiritual life, eternal life, but let us not rule out the thought that He may also impart more abundant physical life as well. In fact, it seems that God is interested in the whole man, not just souls. A soul without a body cannot carry on His work here on earth. He came to save mankind, not just souls. Born-again Christians form the body of Christ through which He does His work today. If you had a servant working for you would you rather have one who was strong and healthy or one who was weak and sickly?

Jesus Christ is the Source of life. He is the Creator who gave men life in the beginning. He said, "I am the resurrection, and the life" (John 11:25). His life is completely free from all disease and contamination. This is the life that He imparts to us, just as branches receive their life from the vine. We are also exhorted to let the Word of God abide in us. Jesus said, "The words that I speak unto you, they are spirit, and they are life" (John 6:63). Having the Source of life within us, it is only normal to expect to have more abundant life, both spiritually and physically.

Many of our illnesses seem to be the result of things that occurred to us in the past, perhaps even in early childhood. The psychiatrist may bring some of these causes to the surface, but he often finds that he is unable to effect the needed healing. Many who pray for the sick today are stressing the importance of "inner healing." Thank God that the Christ who dwells within is well able to cope with any situation and bring about that "inner healing" that is so necessary.

We have already noted that the one who brought sin and sickness into the world was the devil and that Christ came to destroy the works of the devil. Remember at all times that "greater is he that is in you, than he that is in the world" (1 John 4:4). Through Christ we can be more than conquerors. Through Him we can live temperate lives, achieve emotional balance, and enjoy His divine protection and the continual indwelling presence of the very Source of life! Yes, a real Christian should be the healthiest and happiest person in the world.

11

God Wants to Heal

No one who believes in the God of the Bible and His involvement in the affairs of men today doubts the ability of the Lord to heal physical illness. We all know that God is able to heal, and many have seen recoveries that medical science cannot explain. The biggest barrier to faith is the question: "Is it God's will to heal?" or "Who does God want to heal?" We can claim the power of God only when we know the will of God.

The Episcopal Church appointed a commission of scholars to make a thorough study of the subject of divine healing. After 3 years of study and research they said in their report: "The healing of the sick by Jesus was done as a revelation of God's will for man." They also stated: "No longer can the Church pray for the sick with the faith destroying, qualifying phrase 'If it be Thy will.' "[1]

In this chapter I would like to give seven reasons why I believe God wants to heal those who are sick.

Christ Came to Do the Will of the Father

(1) *Christ came to earth to do the will of the Father, and He healed all who came to Him for healing.* Christ was perfectly united with the Father, and it is inconceivable that He would go against the will of God. This will was not always pleasant, but Christ was willing to undergo even the death of the cross. In Hebrews 10, after we read of the insufficiency of the animal sacrifices, we find these words, "Then said I, Lo, I come (in the volume of

the book it is written of me) to do thy will, O God" (v. 7). If He was willing to pay the supreme sacrifice to do the will of the Father, surely He would not go against His will in smaller things. In John 6:38 He says, "For I came down from heaven, not to do mine own will, but the will of him that sent me." And in John 8:29 Jesus tells us, "I do always those things that please him." God himself testified that He was pleased with the work of His Son. Would He do this if Christ had been violating His will by healing those that it was not the will of the Father to heal?

Who did Christ heal? Let us look again at the record. In Matthew 8:16 it says: "When the even was come, they brought unto him many that were possessed with devils: and he cast out the spirits with his word, and *healed all that were sick*." Matthew 9:35 says: "And Jesus went about all the cities and villages, teaching in their synagogues, and preaching the gospel of the kingdom, and healing *every sickness and every disease* among the people." In Matthew 12:15 we read: "But when Jesus knew it, he withdrew himself from thence: and great multitudes followed him, and *he healed them all*." Look at Matthew 14:35, 36: "And when the men of that place had knowledge of him, they sent out into all that country round about, and brought unto him all that were diseased; and besought him that they might only touch the hem of his garment: and *as many as touched were made perfectly whole*." There are other such passages, in fact, there are 12 references that state Jesus Christ healed *all* or *every one*, and it is strongly implied in 11 more. Surely this is convincing evidence that God wants to heal. If we had no other proof of His will this should be enough.

Christ Came to Destroy the Works of the Devil

(2) *Christ came to destroy the works of the devil, and sickness is one of his works*. When God finished the work of Creation, it is recorded: "And God saw everything that he had made, and, behold, it was very good" (Genesis 1:31). Man was made in the image of God to have fellowship with God. Satan came and marred the image of God

in man. Sin, sickness, and death came into the world
through Satan. God does not want His image marred,
spiritually or physically, and so He provided an atonement. Jesus Christ brought back to mankind the benefits
lost through the Fall. John the apostle tells us specifically: "For this purpose the Son of God was manifested, that
he might destroy the works of the devil" (1 John 3:8).
Note that it is the *works* and not *work*. Sin and sickness
are both included. Sickness is portrayed in the Bible as an
unnatural condition, a condition that should be changed.

In Acts 10:38 Peter tells those of Cornelius' household:
"How God anointed Jesus of Nazareth with the Holy
Ghost and with power: who went about doing good, and
healing all that were oppressed of the devil; for God was
with him." Don't forget that it is the devil who oppresses,
and Christ is the One who came to set us free.

There is an interesting story in Luke 13 of a woman
whose back was bent severely for 18 years. Jesus healed
her. He was then criticized by the religious leaders because this miracle had been done on the Sabbath Day. In
Christ's reply He said, "Ought not this woman, being a
daughter of Abraham, whom Satan hath bound, lo, these
eighteen years, be loosed from this bond on the sabbath
day?" (v. 16). Note that she was "a daughter of Abraham." Jesus said so. There were others that claimed to
be children of Abraham but Jesus told them they were not
(John 8:33-40). She was one of the elect, but bound by a
"spirit of infirmity." Christ, who came to proclaim liberty
to the captives, set her free from this physical deformity.

"The last enemy that shall be destroyed is death" (1 Corinthians 15:26). Satan brought sin. Sin brought sickness
and death. Christ came to destroy the works of the devil,
so we can confidently expect Him to heal our sicknesses
now. He has already freed His people from spiritual death
and eventually will do away with physical death as
well. Thank God for our all-conquering Saviour!

No Favoritism With God

(3) *Christ expressly stated that it was His will to heal
one person. There is no favoritism with God.* Only once
in the New Testament do we find anyone who questioned

the will of Christ to heal. This was an outcast from society, a leper. He had to stay at a distance from other people, and when anyone came near he was to cry aloud, "Unclean! Unclean!" He had nothing to recommend him to Christ. He had nothing to offer Him—no payment, no reward. Would the great Teacher and Healer have mercy on one whom all others rejected? He did not doubt the ability of Jesus to heal him, although his disease was considered incurable. But would He do it for him? The leper determined to try. He came near to the Master. A throng surrounded Him. If the poor leper had been discovered in the midst of the multitude, he would doubtless have been severely punished for breaking the law that segregated all who had this loathsome disease. Coming near to the Lord the leper worshiped Him and said, "Lord, if thou wilt, thou canst make me clean. And Jesus put forth his hand, and touched him, saying, I will; be thou clean. And immediately his leprosy was cleansed" (Matthew 8:2, 3).

The leper had no way of knowing the will of the Lord and therefore had a right to question it. When the Lord said, "I will; be thou clean," that settled the matter. He did not doubt anymore and was immediately healed. We are similar to this leper in some ways. We do not really have anything to offer the Lord; no real merit of our own. The cleansing (or healing) of the leper, however, did not depend on his merit but on the very nature of the Healer. Christ healed because it was a part of His very nature. He was continually fulfilling the will of His Father and destroying the pain, anguish, and misery brought into this world by the devil.

Is there any reason to believe that the Lord was willing to heal that leper and does not want to heal the sick today? The Bible teaches that there is no favoritism with God. Peter said: "Of a truth I perceive that God is no respecter of persons" (Acts 10:34). Paul confirms this truth: "For there is no respect of persons with God" (Romans 2:11). James teaches that it is sinful to have respect of persons (James 2:1-9). This being true, I believe that if God wills to heal some He wills to heal all who come to Him. True, all are not healed, because all do not meet the conditions. God is "not willing that any should perish" (2 Peter 3:9).

Yet men do perish. Why? Because they will not meet God's conditions. If God was willing to heal the leper and thousands of others in the days when Jesus was here on earth visibly, then He must be willing to heal now. If not, He would be showing respect of persons and favoritism. This we cannot believe of our God. The leper did not know God's will and questioned it. We know God's will. It has been plainly revealed in His Word. We have no right to question what He has revealed.

God Wants to Give Good Things

(4) *As a merciful Father, God wants to give good things to His children.* The inspired Psalmist tells us: "Like as a father pitieth his children, so the Lord pitieth them that fear him" (Psalm 103:13). Jesus compared the imperfect love of earthly fathers to the perfect love of our Heavenly Father and said: "If ye then, being evil, know how to give good gifts unto your children, how much more shall your Father which is in heaven give good things to them that ask him?" (Matthew 7:11). David wrote: "When my father and my mother forsake me, then the Lord will take me up" (Psalm 27:10). God is a good God. James tells us: "Every good gift and every perfect gift is from above, and cometh down from the Father of lights, with whom is no variableness, neither shadow of turning" (James 1:17).

Can you think of cancer as a good gift sent to you by a loving Heavenly Father? If you were a cancer victim and had been suffering its torture for a long time, you could certainly believe that divine healing would be an excellent gift! The fact that God made a covenant with His children and was willing to take away all their sicknesses if they would walk in His ways certainly reveals that God wants His children to be well and healthy. (See Exodus 15:26; 23:25; Deuteronomy 7:12-15.) God wants us to be in good health spiritually and physically, and He even desires to bless us materially. The inspired writing of the apostle John puts it this way: "Beloved, I wish above all things that thou mayest prosper and be in health, even as thy soul prospereth" (3 John 2).

In the case of the Syrophoenician woman who came to Christ to get healing for her daughter, Christ referred to healing as "the children's bread" (Mark 7:27). In other words, it is something that a child has a right to expect. In fact, Jesus himself taught us to pray, "Give us this day our daily bread" (Matthew 6:11). If you are His child you have a right to ask the Father for healing and health.

Christ Revealed as Our Healer

(5) *Christ has revealed himself as our Healer.* We have already referred to the healing pact God made with His people and the revelation of His name Jehovah-Rapha (Exodus 15:26). The tense used in the last clause is the present and can be translated, as Dr. Young has put it: "I the Lord am healing thee." On this subject Dr. A. B. Simpson comments:

> This is the aspect of divine healing which the Apostle Paul so frequently emphasizes. It is not a mere fact or incident occurring occasionally in life, but it is a life of constant, habitual dependence upon Christ for the body; moment by moment abiding in Him for our physical, as well as spiritual need, and taking His resurrection life and strength for every breath and every step.[2]

There can be no better physician than the One who made us and gave us life. He promised to take away *sickness* from His people (Exodus 23:25). He kept His promise (Psalm 105:37). Not one feeble person among them! He is able and willing to do the same today for those that put their trust in Him and walk in His ways.

The Psalmist tells us we should not forget any of the benefits the Lord offers us. He says that the Lord forgives all our iniquities (sins) and heals all our diseases (Psalm 103:3). The word *all* is just as inclusive when it refers to sickness as it is when it refers to iniquities. He is the Healer of soul and body and can do a complete job. There is none like our Great Physician.

One further thing to note on the passage of Exodus 15:26—this is not just an ordinary promise or a "spur of the moment" decision. In verse 25, after telling of the healing of the bitter waters at Marah, it says: "There he made for them a statute and an ordinance, and there he

proved them." The promise of healing is then given together with the conditions. Notice that this is an ordinance, just like baptism is an ordinance. It is a covenant
with His people, and His Word says: "My covenant will I
not break, nor alter the thing that is gone out of my lips"
(Psalm 89:34). He can be depended on to keep His part of
the covenant.

Christ Bore Our Sicknesses

(6) *Christ bore our sicknesses; therefore, we do not
have to bear them.* We have already covered this subject
in chapter 4 so we will not enlarge upon it further at this
point. However, it is very important to keep in mind the
reason why the Lord bore the penalty for our sins and
sicknesses. It was so we would not have to bear them. We
can be free from the condemnation and punishment for
our sins by His death on Calvary, and we can be healed
through accepting the freedom purchased for us by His
stripes. "By whose stripes ye were healed" (1 Peter 2:24).

Jesus Christ Is the Same Today

(7) *"Jesus Christ the same yesterday, and today, and
for ever"* (Hebrews 13:8). We have pointed out that God
is perfect and that any change from perfection would have
to be toward imperfection. This is why our God is im-
mutable, unchanging. In James 1:17 the American Standard Version reads as follows: "Every good gift and every
perfect gift is from above, coming down from the Father
of lights, with whom can be no variation, neither shadow
that is cast by turning." Jesus Christ is God and He does
not change. When one doubts that Jesus Christ heals today he questions one of two things—either His ability or
His willingness. Most Christians do not question the
ability of the Lord to do the supernatural in our day.
Then it must be His willingness that they question.

Suppose you are the father of a sick child who is about
10 years old. You hear the child talking to one of his
friends, and he says: "I know my father would take away
all my pain and fever. He would make me quit hurting

completely in a minute if he only could. But he can't."
This would pain you, but you would not hold it against
the child simply because he questioned your ability. But
suppose the boy says, "I know that my father has special
powers and he can heal all kinds of sickness. He could
take away all my pain and fever and make me well in a
minute, if only he wanted to. But I'm afraid he doesn't
like me well enough, maybe he doesn't want me to be
well." To think that your child believed you didn't love
him enough to want him to be well would cut you to
the heart! You would a thousand times rather he would
doubt your power than your love! Jesus Christ is the
same. He is still the Great Physician. Do you doubt His
power or His love?

To sum it up, I believe it is God's will to heal all who
come to Him for healing because:

(1) Christ came to do His Father's will and healed all
    who came to Him.
(2) Christ came to destroy the works of the devil. This
    includes sin and sickness.
(3) Christ said it was His will to heal one. There is no
    favoritism with Him.
(4) As a merciful Father, God wants to give good things
    to His children.
(5) He has revealed himself as our Healer.
(6) He bore our sicknesses; therefore, we do not have
    to bear them.
(7) Jesus Christ never changes. He is the same yester-
    day, today, and forever.

On the basis of the above facts, I feel that the following
statement is a safe assumption: "So far as the ultimate will
of God is concerned, it may be maintained that it is always
His will to heal, and the request for healing and the
exercise of faith are always in order."[3]

12

Hindrances to Healing

God does not want souls to be lost. He does not want any to perish. He wants all to repent and be saved (Ezekiel 18:32; 2 Peter 3:9). The fact that many do perish does not mean God does not want to save. In the same manner, God wants to heal His children, and the fact that some do not receive their healing does not mean He has changed His mind.

We are told that Thomas Edison made several thousand experiments before he found the right way to produce an incandescent bulb. The fact that he failed a hundred times or a thousand times still did not prove electricity could not be used for producing an efficient light. He learned from his failures and kept at it until he succeeded.

Never let the enemy make you think you should give up because some are not healed in answer to prayer. The light bulb is a blessing. I am glad Edison didn't give up! Divine healing and health can be brought to many through our prayers if we determine not to give up.

No physician can guarantee results if the patient does not follow directions. God has given some clear instructions in His Word for those who want His healing or any answer to prayer. Some say, "When everything else fails, try reading the directions." This seems to be the way many people go about seeking healing and blessings from God. Let's get the directions first!

Ignorance of God's Word

Ignorance of God's Word is very often a hindrance to our prayers. A person may be well acquainted with the Word of God on salvation and some other subjects and yet be ignorant of God's promises to heal. We must know what God has promised, what He wants to do, before we can have faith for the desired results. Remember that faith comes through the Word of God. Go over the Scripture passages given in the previous chapters of this book. Study them carefully in their context. Feed on the Word, and your faith will grow. Don't be cheated out of a part of your inheritance by not knowing what has been left you in His will.

Doubting the Word

Doubting the Word brings defeat. Listen to the comparison Paul makes in Hebrews 4:2: "For unto us was the gospel preached, as well as unto them: but the word preached did not profit them, not being mixed with faith in them that heard it." Here is a clear statement that those who hear the message of the gospel must believe or else the gospel will do them no good. It is the "power of God unto salvation to every one that believeth" (Romans 1:16), but it will bring no blessing to those who reject it through unbelief. God is able, faithful, and truthful. Trust Him fully. Unbelief kept the Children of Israel from entering the Promised Land (Hebrews 3:19). Unbelief makes people turn away from God (v. 12). Unbelief hinders the healing power of Christ (Matthew 13:58). The unbelieving will be in hell (Revelation 21:8).

Wrong Motives

Wrong motives can hinder one from receiving the desired blessing. James says: "Ye ask, and receive not, because ye ask amiss, that ye may consume it upon your lusts" (4:3). Why do you wish to be healed? Is it simply the desire to be free from pain and to enjoy life more? Do you have a sincere desire to glorify God through a testimony of His healing power? Do you want to be a more efficient worker for the Lord? I doubt that the Lord would be interested in healing your lame foot so that you might dance better! Or prolonging a life dedicated entirely to worldly pleasure. In fact, we should want the Healer more than the healing, the Blesser more than the blessing.

Misplaced Faith

Misplaced faith can hinder our healing. Many have faith in some particular shrine, chapel, or holy place. Jesus told the Samaritan woman that the place was not the important thing, but worshiping God in spirit and in truth (John 4:19-24). Some think that if they can only get to the evangelist that feels the power of God in his right hand, or to the one who can diagnose their illness, they will be healed. Some want to get to the shrine of the image of the virgin that sheds tears; others want to get to the evangelist who seems to be having the greatest success. What is wrong with all this? Simply that the faith of the sufferer is not in the promises of God, God's provision for our healing, but in some person, place, or object.

Just as it is possible to have faith in another person's faith, it is also possible to have faith in your own faith. A person is led to believe that if he can just manage to work up enough faith he will receive his healing. The healing will be something like a prize for having so much faith. This would place healing on the basis of merit. We would obligate God by our strong faith! We can readily see that this is not Biblical. The Bible teaches that all we receive from God comes by His grace, even the faith for salvation!

Trusting in Merit

Trusting in merit is a way in which many are misled. People believe they will be healed because of what they are or do. We are healed because of what God is and what He has done. He is a merciful, compassionate Father who delights in showing mercy to His children (Psalm 103:13; Micah 7:18).

Sin

Sin is a hindrance to all prayer. The existence of sickness in this world is a direct result of sin. This does not mean, however, that every sickness is a direct result of some sin. In the case of the man born blind, Jesus said that this was not the result of sin on his part or on the part of his parents (John 9:1-3). At the same time, we should recognize that sometimes there can be a direct cause-and-effect relationship between sin and sickness. Jesus told the crippled man that He met and healed at the pool of Bethesda, "Behold, thou art made whole: sin no more, lest a worse thing come upon thee" (John 5:14). In the instructions for praying for the sick given by James, he adds, ". . . if he have committed sins, they shall be forgiven him" (James 5:15). This would seem to indicate that sin could be a causative factor in the sickness.

An unforgiving spirit definitely hinders our prayers. The Lord makes it very plain that if we do not forgive others we cannot expect to be forgiven (Matthew 6:14). Foretelling the blessings of the future kingdom, the prophet Isaiah says: "And the inhabitant shall not say, I am sick: the people that dwell therein shall be forgiven their iniquity" (Isaiah 33:24). Forgiveness, and then healing, is the order.

A great healing *en masse* took place in the days of King Hezekiah. In 2 Chronicles 30:20 we find: "And the Lord hearkened to Hezekiah, and healed the people." A good deal of preparation went before this blessing. The land was cleansed from idolatry (2 Kings 18:4); the temple was cleaned up (2 Chronicles 29:16); and they celebrated a great Passover festival (2 Chronicles 30). When idolatry and sin had been removed and the people had repented and made sacrifices to the true God, healing came for all.

There are so many sins that it would be impossible to catalog them all here. Lack of harmony between husband and wife can cause prayers to go unanswered (1 Peter 3:7). We often wonder why there are not more manifestations of the power of God to convince our skeptical generation. Perhaps the word of the prophet Isaiah may be applicable to us: "Behold, the Lord's hand is not shortened, that it cannot save; neither his ear heavy, that it cannot hear: but your iniquities have separated between you and your God, and your sins have hid his face from you, that he will not hear" (Isaiah 59:1, 2). David knew what sin and failure were, and he also knew the blessing of forgiveness. He was speaking from experience when he said: "If I regard iniquity in my heart, the Lord will not hear me" (Psalm 66:18). God's Word declares: "He that covereth his sins shall not prosper: but whoso confesseth and forsaketh them shall have mercy" (Proverbs 28:13).

It is most important that we prepare our hearts to seek the Lord for healing or any of His blessings. Anything that brings condemnation to our heart will hinder us from appropriating God's promises. We should examine carefully our relationship with God and with our fellowman. Forgiveness and cleansing are available through the infinite grace of our Lord.

Rebellion

Rebellion against the will of God is another thing that often hinders healing. Of course rebellion is sin. In fact, it is basic to most sins and the sin that caused the fall of Lucifer and his angels. Many Christians testify to the fact that they could not get victory over their illness because they did not want to do what God was asking them to do. Sometimes it was simply asking forgiveness of one they had wronged. Sometimes it was a surrender of their life to God for the ministry or missionary service. When they at last yielded to the Lord, they received instantaneous healing. If we want God's best for our lives we must allow Him to direct our steps.

Abuse of the Laws of Health

Abuse of the laws of health is another factor that hinders our healing and health. This has been discussed in the chapter on causes of sickness, but it is well to remind ourselves that we are still mortal beings subject to the laws of nature the same as other people. We cannot continually overeat, partake of harmful things, fail to get the rest our body demands, and expect God to make an exception and keep us strong and healthy for many years of service to Him. It is an indictment against us that so many ministers have nervous breakdowns, heart attacks, and other similar illnesses that incapacitate them for service, when God wants us well and strong so we may be able to help others.

Lack of Prayer and Fasting

Lack of prayer and fasting can be a hindrance and keep us from victory. In Mark 9:14-29 we have an example. The disciples had prayed for a boy with a dumb spirit, but he had not been healed. When Jesus came He discerned the true cause and cast out the evil spirit, and the boy was healed. Later when they were alone with the Lord the disciples asked why they had not been successful. They had been given power to cast out demons and had successfully done so before this. Why, then, were they not able to deliver this lunatic boy? Jesus told them: "This kind can come forth by nothing, but by prayer and fasting" (v. 29). Jesus had just come from the Mount of Transfiguration, one of the greatest spiritual experiences imaginable. He was in direct touch with the Father. No doubt He had been fasting while He was alone in the mountain. He was prepared.

We should learn from this example that our "mountaintop" experiences are for the purpose of preparing us for confrontations with the enemy. For him to challenge us after such an experience is not strange.

What about fasting? What is the object of a fast? Fasting is mentioned often in the Bible, and it seems that there were different manners of fasting. Daniel, a man greatly beloved of the Lord, said: "And I set my face unto the Lord God, to seek by prayer and supplications, with fasting, and sackcloth, and ashes: and I prayed unto the Lord my God, and made my confession . . ." (Daniel 9:3, 4). On another occasion he said that he ate no pleasant bread and abstained from all meat and wine for 3 full weeks while he was mourning before the Lord (10:2, 3). The purpose seems to have been to withdraw from the regular activities and dedicate himself entirely to seeking God in repentance and humility. Later, it seems that the fast became somewhat of a ritual. The Pharisee who was praying in the temple was rather boastful of the fact that he fasted twice a week (Luke 18:12). The Lord told of those who hypocritically wanted everyone to know that they were fasting so people would think them very religious (Matthew 6:16-18). Jesus condemned this practice, but did not condemn fasting.

In times of great crises and dangers, a whole nation would be called upon to fast and pray. (See 2 Chronicles 20:3; Ezra 8:21; Esther 4:16; Jeremiah 36:9; Joel 1:14, 15; Jonah 3:5.) Nevertheless, fasting itself was not pleasing to the Lord if the people did not do His will. Isaiah 58 makes this clear.

Fasting and prayer with true humility and repentance can bring rich spiritual reward. This is the purpose of the fast. When we get everything else out of the way, God can get through to us and communicate with us. His sacred presence will make a tremendous difference in our ministry. How much do you want to hear from the Lord? Job said, "I have esteemed the words of his mouth more than my necessary food" (Job 23:12).

Some have mistakenly believed that fasting is a sacrifice that obliges God to do certain things. This is misleading and dangerous. We cannot put God under obligation to us no matter what we do. It is impossible! Fasting is for the purpose of getting nearer to God. Signs and wonders may follow our fasts, yet they are not a result of the fast itself, but of our being more filled with the Spirit and the power of God.

Lack of Intense Desire

Lack of intense desire can be the reason many do not receive healing. James says: "The effectual *fervent* prayer of a righteous man availeth much" (James 5:16). The word *fervent* used here is the same word from which we get our word *fever*. We should not be prayed for just to see what will happen. We should be fully convinced of God's will and desire earnestly, sincerely, and intensely the miracle that will bring glory to God in our life.

Looking at Symptoms

Looking at symptoms sometimes causes one to lose the healing that should have been his. Very often the sick person feels immediate relief at the moment prayer is offered, and he believes that he is well. A short while afterward some of the old symptoms return. The tendency then is to think, "Well, I guess I'm not healed after

all. I thought I was, but now I feel the same pains again."
What is happening? The person is going by feeling and
not by faith; looking at symptoms, rather than looking to
Christ and His promises. This is really a trick of the devil
to try to defeat us and keep us from the blessing God
wants to give. We are told: "Resist the devil, and he will
flee from you" (James 4:7). Resist him with "the sword of
the Spirit, which is the word of God" (Ephesians 6:17).
Tell Satan, "It is written, by His stripes I was healed." We
should also realize that some healings are not instantaneous, but are none the less real.

Concluding this chapter on hindrances to healing, we
should perhaps consider one more aspect. "It is appointed unto men once to die" (Hebrews 9:27). Death is
the last enemy that will be subjected to Christ (1 Corinthians 15:26). Our physical bodies are still mortal and,
therefore, subject to death. Death has lost its sting for the
Christian (v. 55). Death to him is not a tragedy. It should
be the glorious finale of a victorious life. "Precious in the
sight of the Lord is the death of his saints" (Psalm 116:
15). There comes a time for us to leave this earthly tabernacle. Paul even longed to depart and be with Christ.
However, there is nothing in the Bible to indicate that
the death of a child of God will be the direct result of some
incurable disease.

J. Robertson McQuilkin, former missionary to Japan
and now President of Columbia Bible College, was asked
by an elderly Christian, "Why does God let us get old and
weak?" His answer was:

I'll tell you my theory. I think God has planned the strength and
beauty of youth to be physical. But the strength and beauty of age is
spiritual. We gradually lose the strength and beauty that is temporary
so we'll be sure to concentrate on the strength and beauty which is
forever. And so we'll be eager to leave the temporary, deteriorating
part of us, and be truly homesick for our eternal Home. If we stayed
young and strong and beautiful, we might never want to leave! It's sad
to see people struggle so frantically to preserve the physical, never
developing the strength and beauty of spirit. In the end they are left
with neither—weak and impoverished in body *and* spirit.[1]

In our earnest quest for physical health we must never
neglect the one thing that will matter when we finish our
earthly course—the welfare of our eternal soul.

There was given to me a thorn in the flesh. 2 Corinthians 12:7.
Drink no longer water, but use a little wine for thy stomach's sake.
1 Timothy 5:23

13

Paul's Thorn, Timothy's Wine, and Other Questions

The doctrine of divine healing brings many questions to mind. Some are questions raised by sincere believers who simply want a clear answer, something that will strengthen their faith and dispel their doubts. Some of the questions are used by those who oppose the doctrine and seem to think that there is clear scriptural evidence against it. In this chapter we wish to discuss briefly some of the more common questions or objections that are proposed.

Paul's Thorn in the Flesh

The Biblical account of Paul's thorn is found in 2 Corinthians 12:7-10, and is as follows:

And lest I should be exalted above measure through the abundance of the revelations, there was given to me a thorn in the flesh, the messenger of Satan to buffet me, lest I should be exalted above measure. For this thing I besought the Lord thrice, that it might depart from me. And he said unto me, My grace is sufficient for thee: for my strength is made perfect in weakness. Most gladly therefore will I rather glory in my infirmities, that the power of Christ may rest upon me. Therefore I take pleasure in infirmities, in reproaches, in necessities, in persecutions, in distresses for Christ's sake: for when I am weak, then am I strong.

Many take this passage to mean that the apostle Paul had a sickness that was sent by the Lord to afflict him, that he prayed three times for its removal and was refused by the Lord. This, they claim, shows that we cannot expect healing in some cases. They believe the Lord has sent the sickness for a purpose and we should not pray for its removal. Let us examine some of the facts in this case.

First, note well that there is no proof that Paul's "thorn in the flesh" was a sickness of any kind. The expression was not unique. In Numbers 33:55 we read: "But if ye will not drive out the inhabitants of the land from before you; then it shall come to pass, that those which ye let remain of them shall be pricks in your eyes and thorns in your sides, and shall vex you in the land wherein ye dwell." Joshua told the Israelites that if they mixed with the heathen, idolatrous people of the land, these people would become "scourges in your sides, and thorns in your eyes" (Joshua 23:13). Paul did not say that his "thorn" was a disease. He said it was a "messenger of Satan" and even told why this came about. The word here translated "messenger" is translated more than a hundred times in the New Testament as "angel."

Note what the task of this angel of Satan was. It was to "buffet" Paul. To "buffet" means to "strike blow after blow." In this same epistle Paul had just concluded a long recital of the things that he had suffered for the gospel's sake—shipwreck, imprisonments, perils of every description, beatings, stonings, and so on. These were doubtless some of the buffetings referred to.

Why did Paul have to suffer so much? For one thing, he was reaping what he had sown. He had been a most zealous persecutor of the Church and now he was reaping. In fact, when the Lord asked Ananias to go pray for Saul of Tarsus immediately after his conversion, he told him: "I will show him how great things he must suffer for my name's sake" (Acts 9:16). Second, this suffering was to keep him humble. God gave such an abundance of revelations to Paul that he could easily have become exalted had it not been for the humiliations that the Lord made him go through. If you think that you have a "thorn in the flesh" that the Lord doesn't want to take away, you might ask yourself: "What great revelations of divine wisdom and power have I had, what outstanding ministry, so that the Lord has to use these measures to keep me humble?"

In my opinion it is completely unwarranted in the Scriptures to think and say that Paul's thorn was a loathsome, oriental eye disease. God had healed Paul's blind eyes at Damascus. The expression "thorn in the flesh" was merely an illustration, as we have seen. So also was the statement that he made to the Galatians: "I bear you record, that, if it had been possible, ye would have plucked out your own eyes, and have given them to me" (Galatians 4:15). This did not mean that he had need of an eye transplant, but simply meant that they would have done anything in their power for Paul.

It is true that Paul told them in a previous verse of the same chapter: "Ye know how through infirmity of the flesh I preached the gospel unto you at the first" (v. 13). The word *infirmity* can be translated "sickness," but is often used as "frailty" or "weakness." Some believe that Paul's first visit was right after he had been stoned in Lystra and left for dead. He then arose and continued to preach in the towns of the province of Galatia. If this is true, it would be easy to understand how he would have been weak "at the first." There is no indication that he continued weak.

Whatever you think of Paul's thorn, it is well to note that it did not hinder his faith. In Ephesus "God wrought special miracles by the hands of Paul" (Acts 19:11). It did not hinder his labors. "I labored more abundantly than they all" (1 Corinthians 15:10). It did not hinder his ministry. (Read Romans 15:17-20.) He accepted the buffeting as God's will and even gloried in tribulation.

Timothy's Wine

Practically every drunkard in the country knows that Paul told Timothy to take a little wine for his stomach's sake. It may be the only verse of the Bible that they know anything about, but they are quick to quote it to defend their actions.

In many areas of the world even today the water is not safe to drink. Many world travelers can testify to this. In Timothy's time it must have been much worse. This could be the reason for his illness and Paul's advice. We must recognize the fact that the Bible severely condemns drunkenness, but does not totally prohibit the use of wine. Many of us feel that the best way to avoid the danger of ever becoming a drunkard is total abstinence. Remember that, "Use a little wine for thy stomach's sake" (1 Timothy 5:23), does not mean, "Drink a lot of alcoholic beverages and destroy your stomach and your health!"

Snake Handlers

In the Great Commission as given in Mark's Gospel, the Lord said: "And these signs shall follow them that believe; In my name shall they cast out devils; they shall speak with new tongues; they shall take up serpents; and if they drink any deadly thing, it shall not hurt them; they shall lay hands on the sick, and they shall recover" (Mark 16:17, 18). Some have interpreted this to mean that Christians should seek opportunities to handle poisonous snakes and thus prove to the world the power of the Lord and the effectiveness of their own faith. These people may be very sincere, but their faith has not always been equal to the occasion. The result has been a lot of unfavorable publicity and much discredit to the gospel.

We believe that Paul demonstrated the true meaning of this passage when he was bitten by a deadly viper, shook it off into the fire, and felt no harmful effects. It was a very convincing sign to those who saw it. We do not know of any record of early Christians trying to prove their faith in this manner.

When the devil tried to get Christ to go against all the laws of nature and throw himself down from the pinnacle of the temple, even quoting from the Scriptures to justify such action, the Lord answered: "It is written again, Thou shalt not tempt the Lord thy God" (Matthew 4:7). We believe that handling serpents would fall in the same category. We do not know of any who go around drinking poison to show their faith, and yet this is mentioned in the same verse.

Perhaps the confrontation with serpents may have a symbolic meaning. Satan is called "that old serpent, which is the Devil" (Revelation 20:2). When Jesus sent the Seventy out to preach, He told them, "Behold, I give unto you power to tread on serpents and scorpions, and over all the power of the enemy; and nothing shall by any means hurt you" (Luke 10:19).

Does the Devil Heal?

Many are puzzled by healings that are not done in the name of Christ or do not honor Him. How do we explain alleged healings (some undoubtedly real), by Christian Scientists, spiritists, and those of other cults?

We have already noted that many illnesses are psychosomatically induced. Consequently, a change of attitude toward the affliction could bring relief and healing. This would hold true in many cases of "faith" healing. The faith would not have to be in Jesus Christ, it could be in almost anything.

There is another aspect, however, that should be considered. If the devil can afflict people (and the Bible clearly teaches that he does), he can just as easily quit afflicting them if it is to his advantage to do so. If he can get people to turn from Christ by something that appears to be a supernatural healing, he will be quick to do so. He certainly would not want to see a person healed who would serve and glorify Christ more than ever before. This is one reason he resists so persistently all efforts to receive genuine healing from Christ.

Why Aren't All Healed?

This is perhaps the question most frequently asked, and perhaps the most difficult to answer. Jesus Christ healed all the sick that came to Him for healing. He did not go about healing everyone, whether they asked for healing or not. He healed one man at the pool of Bethesda, but evidently left others with their infirmities. (See John 5:1-13.) In some cases it seems that all the sick who sought the early disciples of Christ were healed (Acts 5:14-16). Why are some not healed today?

In the chapter on hindrances to healing we have shown that there are many things that can keep our prayers from being answered. In some cases we might easily discern the reasons, but in other cases it would be difficult, if not impossible, to do so. There may be wrong motives, misplaced faith, or sin in the life which would hinder our prayers and prevent us from receiving the blessing the Lord wants to give.

In some cases the one seeking healing wants an instantaneous miracle and not just a supernatural healing. If the healing does not come instantly, he thinks his prayer is not answered and loses faith. It has been aptly said, "God's delays are not His denials." Think of how long Abraham believed God. Daniel prayed and was heard of the Lord at the very first, but it took 3 weeks to get the answer (Daniel 10:13).

It seems that sometimes there is a special time for one to receive healing that will bring more glory to God. The man born blind (John 9) was healed "that the works of God should be made manifest in him" (v. 3). However, he suffered blindness for many years before his day finally arrived. If Jesus had gone immediately to Bethany and healed Lazarus of his sickness, it would not have been anything like the miracle of raising him from the dead.

If God has allowed some sickness to come upon us to teach us a lesson, then the sickness may not be removed until we have learned that lesson. The Psalmist said, "It is good for me that I have been afflicted; that I might learn thy statutes" (Psalm 119:71).

Why God does not choose to heal some, we are unable to explain; but we must admit that in the final analysis God is sovereign and His ways are best. When we lament the homegoing of some precious loved one, we are generally more concerned with our loss rather than their gain. To finish our course with joy and enter into the blessings prepared for the faithful is a great triumph and motive of rejoicing.

It is true that some handicapped Christians do more witnessing for Christ than others who are strong and robust. Nevertheless, we believe that it is God's general will for all His children to be well and healthy.

Trophimus Left Sick

Trophimus was a traveling companion of Paul. He was with him on his last trip to Jerusalem. He was a Gentile from Ephesus. Much later Paul wrote to Timothy what was possibly his last epistle. He told of some that had deserted, and others that were working in different places, and then added: "Trophimus have I left at Miletus sick" (2 Timothy 4:20).

Some use this to teach that we cannot always expect to be healed. "Even the apostle Paul could not cure Trophimus," they say. Of course Paul was not the healer. It had to be the work of Jesus Christ. We do not know what hindrances there may have been to keep Trophimus from receiving his healing at this particular time.

Keep in mind, however, that although he was sick at the time of Paul's letter, this does not mean that he was not healed, that the Lord refused to heal him, or that he remained a hopeless invalid the rest of his life.

Epaphroditus was another one of Paul's co-workers. In Philippians 2:25-30 we find that he became sick and was at the point of death, but the Lord raised him up. Since we are told that he ministered to Paul's needs (v. 25), and "for the work of Christ he came nigh unto death, hazarding his life to supply that which was lacking in your service toward me" (v. 30, ASV), some scholars believe that overwork was the cause of his sickness. God had mercy and restored him in answer to prayer. This should show us that regardless of how worthy our work may be, it is possible to overdo and become incapacitated. Many pastors, missionaries, and evangelists have learned this lesson the hard way. We need to use the intelligence the Lord has given us in the care of our bodies, the temples of the Holy Spirit.

Retaining Your Healing

Is it possible to be really healed through divine power and then lose your healing? This is not only possible but does happen quite frequently. After Jesus healed the helpless cripple who had been suffering for 38 years, He gave him this word of caution: "Behold, thou art made whole: sin no more, lest a worse thing come unto thee" (John 5:14).

The return of symptoms of the old sickness is one of the tricks the enemy frequently uses to cause doubt, which in turn causes the loss of the healing. The blessing that is received through faith must be maintained through faith. Keep on believing and praising God for victory. The enemy will have to flee as you stand firmly on the promises of God. Let him know that you belong to Christ. You are God's property and he has no right to trespass. Order him to leave in the name of Jesus.

Do not fail to give glory to God for the healing. Some have failed to give God credit and have lost their healing. Surely He is worthy. Let us give Him the glory that is His just due. Let us confess Him before men, confess Him as Saviour, Healer, and Lord of our life! This is the road not only to healing but to divine health, which is better.

14

Deliverance From Demon Powers

In recent years there has been a tremendous upsurge of interest in Satan, demons, witchcraft, and the occult. The book *The Exorcist* and the film made from the book have greatly stirred the imagination of the public. Many theologians who have deliberately ignored the Biblical teaching on demonology are being forced to take a new look at the subject. This is in complete agreement with Paul's prophecy: "Now the Spirit speaketh expressly, that in the latter times some shall depart from the faith, giving heed to seducing spirits, and doctrines of devils" (1 Timothy 4:1). The scope of this book does not permit a full study of the matter, but we will endeavor to present the role of demonic powers in physical illnesses and the provision made for complete deliverance through Jesus Christ.

What Is a Demon?

The Greek word *daimon* was used in classical writings to refer to a god or a divine power, but in the New Testament it is always used in a bad sense, as referring to an evil spirit. When the word *devil* is used in the singular it refers only to Satan. When it is used in the plural, "devils," it means "demons." Demons, then, are evil spirits that are allied with Satan and helping to carry out his work of rebellion against God.

The Bible does not state clearly just how, where, and when demons had their origin. Some believe them to be the disembodied spirits of a pre-Adamic race that were aligned with Satan, Lucifer, before his fall. Others think that they are fallen angels that were cast out of heaven with Satan when he fell. Both of these theories have some supporting evidence but not enough to be conclusive or dogmatic. Their exact origin is not as important as their nature, their activities, and how to overcome them.

Many kinds of evil spirits are mentioned in the Bible: lying spirits (1 Kings 22:21, 22); jealous spirits (Numbers 5:14); seducing spirits (1 Timothy 4:1); deaf spirits (Mark 9:25); spirits of infirmity (Luke 13:10-17); unclean spirits (Mark 1:23); and others. The Lord did not bother to give us a complete list of demons with their categories and job descriptions. He simply told His followers: "Behold, I give unto you power . . . over *all the power of the enemy;* and nothing shall by any means hurt you" (Luke 10:19). "As spiritual beings, demons are intelligent, vicious, unclean, with power to afflict man with physical hurt, and moral and spiritual contamination."[1] Yet the Lord clearly tells us that we have no reason to fear them because in Christ we are "more than conquerors."

Activities of Demons

It seems that demons have a desire to kill or destroy. The man who brought his devil-possessed son to the Lord told how the boy often fell in the water or fire. Clearly the demon was trying to destroy him. Jesus cast out the demon and set him free (Matthew 17:14-18). The devil binds (Luke 13:16). Christ came to proclaim liberty to those who were bound (Luke 4:18). Jesus said, "The thief cometh not, but for to steal, and to kill, and to destroy: I am come that they might have life, and that they might have it more abundantly" (John 10:10). Christ is the Creator (John 1:1-3; Colossians 1:16). The devil is called Apollyon (the Destroyer) (Revelation 9:11). The wages of sin is death, but the gift of God is life (Romans 6:23). Many of the senseless killings that we read about in the newspapers are doubtless demon inspired. This is also true of many suicides. Sickness brings about death and death is an enemy (1 Corinthians 15:26). Therefore it is not surprising to find demons afflicting people with all manner of sickness and disease.

This does not mean that every time a person becomes sick demons should be cast out of him. It means that sin and Satan are to blame for the origin of sickness, the very germs that produce sickness. The devil still delights in afflicting people today, but his power is limited and the genuine Christian need not fear him or his cohorts.

Strange as it may seem, demon powers can also produce seeming miracles of healing. In 2 Thessalonians 2:9 we are told that the coming of the Antichrist will be " . . . after the working of Satan with all power and signs and lying wonders." In Revelation 16:14 we read of " . . . spirits of devils, working miracles." Speaking of the time immediately preceding His return, the Lord said, "There shall arise false Christs, and false prophets, and shall show great signs and wonders; insomuch that, if it were possible, they shall deceive the very elect" (Matthew 24:24). The False Prophet, who is to deceive the people and cause them to follow the Antichrist, will be a worker of miracles (Revelation 19:20).

The Lord has warned us: "Not every one that saith unto me, Lord, Lord, shall enter into the kingdom of heaven; but he that doeth the will of my Father which is in heaven. Many will say to me in that day, Lord, Lord, have we not prophesied in thy name? and in thy name have cast out devils? and in thy name done many wonderful works? And then will I profess unto them, I never knew you: depart from me, ye that work iniquity" (Matthew 7:21-23). The passage clearly indicates that there will be some who use the name of Jesus Christ to perform wonders, exorcism, and prophetic utterances, but who are still "workers of iniquity." In magic rites, spiritism, and other occult practices, the name of Jesus is often used. Sometimes the names of the Trinity are used. But Jesus said, "By their fruits ye shall know them" (Matthew 7:20).

If demons are able to afflict and cause people to suffer sicknesses and infirmities, they can also stop afflicting when it is to their advantage to do so. This can explain many of the alleged cures of spiritism, Christian Science, Satan worshipers, and other non-Christian groups.

The apostle John tells us not to believe every spirit, but to try the spirits to see if they are of God (1 John 4:1). Not all supernatural things are of God.

Where there is a counterfeit there is a genuine. The powers sought and claimed by the occultists are largely counterfeits of the gifts of the Spirit the Lord gave to His church. If these gifts were in operation in the Church today in the manner and to the extent that God intended, there would be no need for people who are seeking reality to turn to the occult to find a manifestation of the supernatural.

The work or activities of demons are often divided into two categories: (1) demon oppression; and (2) demon possession. This seems to be the progressive order. Some add the category of demon depression.

Demon oppression is the most common and can affect the unwary Christian as well as the unbeliever. Although provision has been made for our perfect liberty and the price of our redemption has been paid, the devil and his agents will encroach upon God's property any time there is an opportunity to do so. God's Word teaches that one who is born of God does not practice sin, that he keeps himself, and the wicked one does not touch him (1 John 5:18). This indicates that if a Christian lowers his guard and permits sin in his life he is leaving an opening for the devil to get in. Satan is always trying to bring about our downfall and will do so if not actively resisted with the "sword of the Spirit, which is the word of God" (Ephesians 6:17). The enemy of our souls uses many means of oppressing and trying to discourage the Christian. Trials, difficulties, opposition, and bodily ailments are some of his methods. Thank God there is victory over every evil power through the finished work of Jesus Christ! The woman who had an ailment in her back and had been bent over and suffered for 18 years was said to have been bound by Satan (Luke 13:16).

Demon possession in the New Testament is sometimes referred to as having a spirit, or a demon, or demons, or an unclean spirit. More often some who suffered physical disease or mental derangement were referred to as "demonized" (*daimonizomenoi*). In demon possession the demon, or demons, take up their abode in an individual and dominate and control him. This may at times result in complete insanity (Matthew 17:15-18; Mark 5:5; Luke 8:35). At times the individual may have extraordinary powers (Acts 16:16-18; 19:16). He may have knowledge of things and speak of things that humanly speaking it would be impossible for him to know (Mark 1:24, 34). Some people may remain docile and nonviolent while demon possessed; others may become violent and even dangerous (Matthew 8:28).

This demon possession is the counterfeit of being possessed by the Spirit of God, the Holy Spirit. A Christian should have extraordinary powers when fully possessed by the Spirit of God. Look at the exploits of Samson and others when "the Spirit of the Lord came upon them." Why do we talk so much about demon possession and so little about being totally possessed by the Holy Spirit?

The number of demons that can inhabit one body seems to be anywhere from one to a legion. In Mark 1:23 we find one unclean spirit in a man. Jesus cast seven demons out of Mary Magdalene (Luke 8:2). The Gadarene demoniac declared that his name was "Legion." This could mean up to 6,000. There were enough to go into 2,000 swine. (See Luke 8:26-33; and Mark 5:1-13.)

Much demon possession is voluntary. There are many people who wish to gain their own ends and will make a pact with the devil himself if that will get them what they wish. In some lands where pagan religions and practices still prevail there is much demon worship and the devotees earnestly seek to be filled with demon power. We were once given a book by some new converts called *The Devil's Own Book*. This book gives in detail what a person should do to have the power of the devil. There is a warning in the front of the book that this is a serious thing and not to be trifled with.

Demon Power—Superstition or Reality?

Some people, and among them some Christians, doubt the existence of demons today and believe the belief in demons is only a remaining vestige of pagan superstition.

Others sincerely question why, if demons really exist, do we have comparatively few in our country? Dr. John L. Nevius was a Presbyterian missionary to China in the 19th century. When he arrived on the field he heard a good deal of talk about demons. He decided that someone should put an end to these superstitious ideas and demonstrate conclusively that all such tales were false. He then began to gather the needed evidence to write a book on the subject. It was not too long before he discovered that there was entirely too much evidence to be brushed aside. The result of his thorough investigation and research was a book that has long been considered one of the best on the subject of demonology. He and his fellow missionaries not only discovered the reality of demons but how to cast them out through prayer and the Word of God.[2] In 1960 the Moody Press published a collection of incidents from around the world called *Demon Experiences in Many Lands.*[3] These varied and sometimes frightening experiences gathered from reliable sources certainly testify to the fact that there is demon power in the world today.

Why have there been so comparatively few such cases in the United States, while they seem to abound in some other areas of the world? It is estimated that there are some 175 million animists in the world. Animists can be defined simply as "spirit worshipers." They believe that there are evil and good spirits everywhere, and that even inanimate objects can have spirits. Their religion is a religion of fear. They must always try to appease the evil spirits, for the good spirits will do you no harm. This leads to demon worship and manifestations of demonic powers.

It has been my observation that where there is a widespread knowledge of and respect for the Word of God there is less manifestation of demons. There has been comparatively little animism in our country and a widespread reverence for the Word of God. However, now that people are rejecting the standards of the Bible and are turning to many pagan religions and practices there is a tremendous upsurge of interest in all forms of the occult, with the result that there is more demonic activity in our day than ever before in the history of our country. We need to be aware of this and be prepared to do battle with the enemy.

We do not believe that a Spirit-filled Christian can be possessed by demons. We cannot serve two masters. Darkness has no fellowship with light. Darkness cannot overcome light. Demons may oppress and afflict, tempt, try to discourage, and otherwise hinder God's work in the life of men, but remember always: "Greater is he that is in you, than he that is in the world" (1 John 4:4).

How Can One Be Delivered From Demonic Powers?

Always remember that the Lord has promised that those who believe in Him shall cast out devils (Mark 16:17). Also He has given us power over all the power of the devil, and nothing shall hurt us (Luke 10:19). Satan is a defeated foe.

At times the gift of discernment of spirits may be used to expose the working of demonic powers. At other times these powers will be plainly evident without any supernatural revelation.

Jesus Christ is our best example in dealing with these satanic powers. He is the "stronger" man who can bind every agent of Satan. In Matthew 8:16 we read: "When the even was come, they brought unto him many that were possessed with devils: and he cast out the spirits with his word, and healed all that were sick."

Other instances of Jesus casting out demons are: Matthew 9:32, 33, a dumb spirit; Matthew 12:22, a blind and dumb spirit; Mark 1:23-27 and Luke 4:33-36, an unclean, foul spirit; Mark 5:1-14, the Gadarene demoniac who was possessed of an unclean spirit; Mark 9:17-27, the boy who had a dumb spirit that produced seizures like epilepsy; and Mark 1:39, unspecified, but throughout all Galilee.

Jesus' word was with authority that was recognized even by demons themselves. His Word still has authority and He has given us the use of it. He said He would do anything that we ask in His name (John 14:13). Jesus promised the power to cast out demons to His followers: Matthew 10:8; Mark 3:15; 16:17; Luke 9:1; 10:19.

This power was successfully exercised by His followers: Mark 6:13; Luke 10:17; Acts 5:16; 8:7, 8; 16:18; 19: 11, 12.

The Holy Spirit anointed Jesus with power to heal the sick and all that were oppressed of the devil (Acts 10:38). The same power of the Holy Spirit was sent to the church of the Lord to abide forever (John 14:16). As long as the Holy Spirit remains with us, will He not do the same type of works that He did for Christ and the disciples?

The Word of God, the name of Jesus, and the power of the Holy Spirit are all we need to be able to successfully cast out evil spirits and bring glorious liberty to those who have been in Satan's bondage.

The Word of God tells us that we can know a doctrine by its fruit (Matthew 7:20). One of the most spectacular, widely known, and best-attested cases of demon possession took place in July 1953 in the Bilibid Prison, Manila, Philippines. Lester Sumrall tells the story in the book *The True Story of Clarita Villanueva*.[4] The case was widely publicized and many medical doctors and professors of medicine examined the girl. It was an irrefutable case of demonic powers. When she was delivered in answer to believing prayer, this astonishing fact was also given wide publicity. Shortly afterwards permission was secured and a large evangelistic campaign was held in which prayer for the sick was emphasized. The result was that thousands of people acknowledged Christ as Saviour, a large church (seating some 3,000) was built in Manila, and a spirit of revival spread to many other parts of the islands.

It is high time that those who follow the Lord Jesus Christ today rise up and resist the devil and take the authority over him and his cohorts that has been provided by our Lord, thus continuing the work that Jesus said the Spirit had anointed Him to do, bringing liberty to the captives and setting free those who are bound and oppressed by the enemy of our souls, that archdeceiver, Satan.

A great multitude followed him, because they saw his miracles which he did on them that were diseased. John 6:2

15

Healing and Evangelism

It is an undeniable fact that the Lord Jesus Christ spent much of His time ministering to the sick. According to Matthew's record: "Jesus went about all the cities and villages, teaching in their synagogues, and preaching the gospel of the kingdom, and healing every sickness and every disease among the people" (Matthew 9:35). There is no record of His ever having prescribed a medicine or using some healing agency to do this work. It was done by faith and through the power of the Holy Spirit.

His ministry was in great demand because He was meeting human needs. Multitudes followed Him. Many came to be healed. No doubt others came out of curiosity, wanting to witness the supernatural healing power. Before criticizing too severely those who believe that divine healing should be emphasized in revival campaigns, perhaps it would be well to take a new look at the ministry of our Lord.

Healing and Evangelism in the Gospels

The church of Jesus Christ has a threefold ministry: (1) to the Lord; (2) to the lost; and (3) to fellow believers. Jesus came to the world to "seek and to save that which was lost" (Luke 19:10). He tells us that we are sent with the same commission (John 20:21). If we are to carry out the last command of our Lord, to preach the gospel to every creature, then mass evangelism is essential. As one writer puts it, "Mass communication of the gospel is absolutely essential to any realistic plan for total world evangelization."[1] It has been stated that the Early Church came closer to evangelizing its world than any succeeding generation has. If this is so, it would be well for us to examine carefully the causes of this success.

Look at the example of our Lord's own ministry. We have already noted that a great deal of His time was devoted to the healing of the sick. At times He and His disciples were in such demand that they could only with difficulty find time to eat. (See Mark 3:20; 6:31.) We know that multitudes of people flocked to the Lord. What was the attraction? "They saw his miracles which he did on them that were diseased" (John 6:2). Everyone is interested in health. Rich or poor, young or old, educated or unlearned, all want to be well. It is easy to get a crowd when the supernatural power of God is working in the healing of the sick.

Not only were the crowds attracted by the miraculous healings, but also they were convinced of the divine origin of Christ and, consequently, of the genuineness of His message. Nicodemus stated it clearly: "Rabbi, we know that thou art a teacher come from God: for no man can do these miracles that thou doest, except God be with him" (John 3:2). Again we read in John 2:23, ". . . many believed in his name, when they saw the miracles which he did." A modern author states it this way: "A single public example of the healing of a blind man can say infinitely more to the masses than a library of books on divine healing."[2]

If we are to get the gospel message to our entire world, we certainly need something to attract and convince the multitudes. Divine healing is a most effective means to this end. God's work should be done in God's way and with God's power. This is the only way to true success.

It has been pointed out in a previous chapter that the healing ministry was not confined to the earthly ministry of our Lord. He gave the same power to the Twelve when He sent them forth to evangelize. He told them: "Heal the sick, cleanse the lepers, raise the dead, cast out devils" (Matthew 10:8). In Luke's account he says: "Then he called his twelve disciples together, and gave them power and authority over all devils, and to cure diseases.

And he sent them to preach the kingdom of God, and to heal the sick" (Luke 9:1, 2). Later the Lord sent out 70 disciples and specifically told them to heal the sick (10:9).

Both of these incidents involved people who had been under the direct ministry of the Lord himself. However, we must not think that such powers are limited to the few who were personally present when the Lord was here on earth. Just before His ascension, the Lord gave His command for world evangelization—the Great Commission. In this commission He said: "These signs shall follow them that believe; In my name shall they cast out devils; . . . they shall lay hands on the sick, and they shall recover" (Mark 16:17, 18). This ministry, then, is now open to all believers.

Healing and Evangelism in the Early Church

Stephen was not an "ordained minister." He was chosen to help take care of some of the less glamorous duties of the church, caring for the poor and the widows. However, Stephen was the first one chosen of the seven deacons, and it was stated of him that he was "a man full of faith and of the Holy Ghost" (Acts 6:5). He was a believer. The result? "And Stephen, full of faith and power, did great wonders and miracles among the people" (v. 8).

Philip was another of the seven deacons. When the church was scattered because of persecution, he went down to Samaria and began to preach Christ. We don't know how eloquent or how effective his preaching ministry was, but he had tremendous results. Why? "The people with one accord gave heed unto those things which Philip spake, hearing and seeing the miracles which he did. For unclean spirits, crying with loud voice, came out of many that were possessed with them: and many taken with palsies, and that were lame, were healed. And there was great joy in that city" (Acts 8:6-8). What an evangelistic campaign! Miracles and signs (v. 13) attracted and convinced the masses. They gave heed to the message, were saved, were baptized, and a little later were filled with the Holy Spirit. Imagine the joy in the homes of ex-paralytics who were now healed and able to enjoy a normal life! Multiply that joy by the number healed and you can readily see why "there was great joy in that city."

The healing ministry of the apostle Peter was very effective in evangelism (Acts 3). The lame man at the temple gate had never walked in all his life. He was now 40 years old and doubtless had given up all hope of ever being anything except a crippled beggar. At Peter's command of faith he was instantly healed. He did not even have to learn to walk! He could stand, leap, and walk. He also praised God, and all the people who saw him were amazed and praised God too. The news of this miracle traveled fast and a multitude soon assembled. Peter took advantage of the opportunity and preached Jesus Christ to them. The result? "Many of them which heard the word believed; and the number of the men was about five thousand" (Acts 4:4). What evangelist would not like to have similar results? Remember that God is glorified when we bear "much fruit" (John 15:8).

In the 9th chapter of Acts we are told of two notable healings which the Lord performed through the apostle Peter. The first was the case of Aeneas. He had been bedfast with paralysis for 8 years. "And Peter said unto him, Aeneas, Jesus Christ maketh thee whole: arise, and make thy bed. And he arose immediately. And all that dwelt at Lydda and Sharon saw him, and turned to the Lord" (vv. 34, 35). Here a whole area turned to the Lord because of a miracle of healing. What a powerful means of evangelism!

The second case was that of a dedicated servant of God generally known as Dorcas. She was well-known and respected for the alms and good works she did for the people. She got sick and died. Peter was in a nearby town, so they sent for him. When he arrived, he knelt and prayed, and then in faith commanded the body to arise. Dorcas was raised from the dead and given back to the saints and widows to whom she had been ministering. What was the result? "And it was known throughout all Joppa; and many believed in the Lord" (Acts 9:42).

The Bible tells us that "God wrought special miracles by the hands of Paul" (Acts 19:11). These miracles greatly helped to turn people to Christ on his missionary journeys. He sums it up for us in Romans 15:18, 19:

> I dare not judge how effectively he has used others, but I know this: He has used me to win the Gentiles to God. I have won them by my message and by the good way I have lived before them, and by miracles done through me as signs from God—all by the Holy Spirit's power. In this way I have preached the full Gospel of Christ all the way from Jerusalem clear over into Illyricum *(Living Bible)*.

Illyricum was situated about where Albania is today. Considering the fact that there was no modern means of communication, no radio or television, no newspapers, or even printing presses, it was most remarkable that one man could have such a wide influence. The power of the Holy Spirit that produced miracles of healing was largely responsible for such success. The same power coupled with the mass media of transportation and communication today can have much greater results.

Although we know very little of the ministry of the other followers of our Lord, the description of the ministry of those mentioned leads us to believe that others had a similar ministry. This is no doubt the reason the gospel spread so rapidly during the apostolic and early postapostolic years.

What we do know is that the same commission has been given to us to carry out. The believing ones were told they would receive power to carry this gospel to the ends of the earth. This power was to come with the reception of the Holy Spirit (Acts 1:8). We have already noted that Christ did His mighty works through the power of the Holy Spirit, as Paul did also. Peter's whole life was transformed when he received the fullness of the Spirit on the Day of Pentecost. Stephen was "full of the Holy Ghost," and so were the other followers of the Lord.

If we have been given the same task to fulfill, would we not be granted the same power to do the work? Spiritual warfare cannot be effectually waged with carnal weapons. The same power is available. The Comforter was sent to abide with us forever (John 14:16). The task is the same—world evangelization. The Holy Spirit is the same. His power is the same. The world's need is the same. Therefore we need only to believe, preach what God's Word says, and see the same results.

It is interesting to note that it was the healing of a beggar at the temple gate that brought such a multitude to faith in Christ. In reading the accounts of healing campaigns in different parts of the world and through personal observation, I have noticed that God often uses similar cases. It seems that it is much more effective as a sign to a greater number of people for some notable miracle to be performed on a person who has been in public view. Everyone knows the beggar who has been on the street daily for so many years! A person equally as handicapped, but cloistered in a private home for years, could be healed and very few people would know about it or believe. Healings are often referred to as "signs." A sign points to something or someone. Divine healing should always point people to Christ.

Healing and Evangelism in the 20th Century

When it comes to the role of divine healing in evangelism in our day, there are so many examples that one is at a loss to know which to choose. Many evangelists with a healing ministry have been mentioned in chapter 8, dealing with the subject of "Healing in the 20th Century." These people have been used in an exceptional manner to get the gospel of Christ to great numbers of people.

Dr. Charles Price conducted many union evangelistic campaigns in large cities. Many churches would cooperate and build a large temporary tabernacle that would seat up to 12,000 people. Miracles of healing would take place and thousands of people would accept Christ as their personal Saviour. He also held campaigns in large municipal auditoriums which would be filled to capacity.

Other evangelists used similar methods. Some used large tents, others football or baseball stadiums. Many people would attend meetings in such public places who were prejudiced against churches, or would not attend a church which was not of their faith. In any case, it was the supernatural, the miraculous healings, that attracted the multitudes. Some of these evangelists were not eloquent speakers, and some had to speak through an interpreter to thousands who could not understand English, but the direct manifestation of the power of the Lord through miracles of healing more than made up for any other inadequacy.

In 1930 Douglas Scott and his wife arrived from England in Le Havre, France. They were on their way to Africa to serve as missionaries, but needed to study French first. He witnessed for the Lord and prayed for some sick folk. The Lord began to heal and save so many that they decided to stay in France. He labored there for over 30 years and helped open churches all over the country. Everywhere he labored there were outstanding healings. The Assemblies of God in France owes much of its growth to divine healing. Prayer for the sick is a regular part of the services in their nearly 500 churches.

The evangelical work among the gypsies of France has been given publicity in the press, radio, and television of Paris. The baptized converts now number well over 17,000 and the work grows continually. How did it all start? Someone gave a tract on healing to a gypsy. Later this gypsy's child became desperately sick. Medical help was to no avail. The mother remembered the tract and had someone read it to her. It told how Jesus Christ heals today and gave the address of the local church. She went to the pastor for prayer. The child was miraculously healed. The parents were converted and later received the Holy Spirit and began to witness to other gypsies. A French pastor, Le Cossec, began to help them. A revival began that has reached all of France and has begun to spread among gypsies of Spain and other countries. You can be sure that divine healing is an important part of their doctrine.

Many wonder why the Pentecostal work in Latin America has made such progress in a relatively short period of time. It is now estimated that at least 60 percent of all evangelicals in Latin America are Pentecostal. I have labored for years in Latin America and have been in practically every one of its countries. Speaking from long observation and experience, I feel sure that one of the prime factors of church growth in that part of the world is their strong faith in and emphasis on the doctrine of divine healing. I have checked this observation with a number of experienced missionaries in Latin America and they concur. It is a shame that so many who are studying church growth today overlook this important detail.

The period of greatest growth of the Pentecostal work in Argentina dates from the great salvation-healing campaign held in Buenos Aires in 1954. Tommy Hicks was the evangelist. The campaign began with 5,000 people assembled in the Atlanta Stadium. After 3 weeks it was moved to the immense stadium of Huracan. Some newspapers and magazines reported an attendance of over 200,000 at a single service. Some 25,000 Bibles were sold, and about the same number of New Testaments. Tens of thousands of people made a public confession of faith during the 8 weeks of revival. Many people received healings and churches were filled with new converts. Missionary L. W. Stokes reports that the churches are still benefitting from this campaign.[3]

The revival in Cuba began in 1950 with a campaign in the ball park of Santiago de Cuba. Only 200 or 300 people came the first night, but before the end of the week there were 15,000 people in each service. Miraculous healings were the drawing card. The leading newspaper gave front-page coverage in the Sunday edition, with pictures and testimonies of those who claimed to be healed. Some subscribers objected and thought the reports of healing were false. The reporter secured names and addresses of others who professed to be healed, looked them up, and after interviewing them published further testimonies!

One of the greatest blessings of the Cuban revival of 1950 to 1951 was that evangelist T. L. Osborn, who was used of God to get things started, did not claim any special gifts or mysterious powers. He placed all the emphasis on simply believing God's Word. Faith in the promises of God was made easy. Many missionaries and national workers were inspired to hold similar campaigns, and we saw the same results—thousands attended, there were many supernatural healings, hundreds were truly converted, and new, vigorous, self-supporting churches were established.

Similar up-to-date reports could be given from all around the world. God is still blessing and "confirming the word with signs following" (Mark 16:20). More preaching of the Word is needed to see more results.

Three Things to Consider

A word of caution might be included here for those who wish to make prayer for the sick an important part of their evangelistic ministry. First, stress salvation. Never fail to let people know that the healing of the soul is far more important than the healing of the body. Second, preach Christ—not yourself and your accomplishments. Build the faith of the seekers in Christ and God's Word, and not in your extraordinary powers or faith. Get them to seek the Healer more than the healing. Third, don't overadvertise. Business firms and manufacturers can be prosecuted for this. It can be dishonest. Genuine healings when the campaign begins are the best advertisement. Demonstrate that God answers prayer and people will come. "O thou that hearest prayer, unto thee shall all flesh come" (Psalm 65:2).

Let him call for the elders of the church; and let them pray over him.
James 5:14

16

Healing in the Local Church

Although divine healing is an excellent aid in evangelization, it should not be confined to evangelistic campaigns. Prayer for the sick is a definite part of the ministry of the local church. The best follow-up for an evangelistic campaign in which healing has been stressed is a local church that practices prayer for the sick and has similar results to those of the campaign. The people who are brought to Christ through healing will readily identify with churches that include prayer for the sick in their regular services.

That the Lord intended physical healing to be a part of the ministry of the Church is proven by two things: His gifts of power to the Church, and the instructions for praying for the sick found in James' epistle.

The gifts of the Holy Spirit are given for the express purpose of edifying the believers, as well as for a sign to the unbelievers. (See 1 Corinthians 12:7; 14:4, 5, 12, 22.) Since we have dealt with the gifts of the Spirit with relation to healing in a previous chapter, we will not go over it again at this point. However, let us keep in mind that these gifts were bestowed on the Church for a purpose. They are to be used in the church. God will be glorified and His cause will be best served as we conform more perfectly to the pattern He has given us to follow.

The New Testament Pattern

The only New Testament instructions given to a sick believer are found in James 5:14-16:

Is any sick among you? let him call for the elders of the church; and let them pray over him, anointing him with oil in the name of the Lord: and the prayer of faith shall save the sick, and the Lord shall raise him up; and if he have committed sins, they shall be forgiven him. Confess your faults one to another, and pray one for another, that ye may be healed. The effectual fervent prayer of a righteous man availeth much.

First, note that these instructions are for the believers. "Is there any sick among you?" Children have rights that outsiders do not possess. God's children can confidently expect healing, which Jesus called "the children's bread" (Mark 7:27).

Next, it should be noted that it is the responsibility of the believer to call for the elders of the church. "Let him call." The congregation should be made aware of this fact. Too often a member becomes sick and never notifies the pastor. Later the same person complains because the pastor did not visit him when he was sick! In the Early Church the terms pastor, elder, and bishop were used interchangeably. It also seems that they had more than one pastor in a local church. These, then, were the ones to be called when a believer was sick.

"Let them anoint him with oil." What is the meaning or significance of the oil? What kind of oil should be used? Is this anointing and prayer to be considered as a sacrament of the church? Should people be anointed for healing outside of the church or in the home of a believer?

A. J. Gordon quotes one of the Early Church fathers, Clement, giving directions for visiting the sick and afflicted as follows: "Let them, therefore, with fasting and prayer, make their intercessions, and not with the well arranged and fitly ordered words of learning, but as men who have received the gift of healing confidently, to the glory of God.[1]

The anointing with oil is significant because of what it represents. J. Nelson Parr explains the anointing in the following manner:

The oil is the symbol of the Holy Spirit, and the anointing with oil has always been the pouring of oil upon the persons, altar or vessels

(Genesis 28:18; 31:13; Leviticus 8:10-12; 1 Samuel 16:13). It will be seen from these passages that the anointing with oil was an act of dedication and consecration, implying on the part of the one anointed complete surrender to God of spirit, soul and body, and also symbolizing the power of the Holy Spirit as the quickener of our mortal bodies (see Romans 8:11).[2]

Some wonder about the type of oil to be used for the anointing. The Greek word used in this passage, as well as in Mark 6:13, is the word commonly used for olive oil. This is the oil generally used in churches that have the practice of anointing and praying for the sick. However, I have known of many cases where people have taken whatever form of oil was available, and their prayers were answered and the sick healed.

The oil itself has no curative power and is not used as a medication of any kind. It simply represents the Holy Spirit who empowered both the Lord and those who followed Him to heal the sick. We are anointed with the Holy Spirit, like Christ in Luke 4:18, and we anoint the ones who come to us for help with the symbol of that same Spirit. A small amount of oil is sufficient as a symbol. Usually the minister puts only a drop of oil upon the forehead of the one to be prayed for. Some make the sign of the cross, although there is no Biblical basis for this, or prohibition either, for that matter.

Laying of hands on the sick is mentioned many times in the Bible. (For example: Matthew 8:15; Mark 5:23; 6:5; 8:23; 16:18; Luke 4:40; 13:13; Acts 9:17.) However, the anointing of the sick with oil is mentioned only twice. Once in the case of the disciples: "And they cast out many devils, and anointed with oil many that were sick, and healed them" (Mark 6:13). The second time it is mentioned in the instructions to the sick in James 5. This does not mean that it was not done at other times. In fact, some infer that it was such a common practice that it was not thought necessary to give detailed instructions. It would seem that the anointing and prayer for the sick in the ministry of the disciples was a part of their public ministry and was not confined to the houses of believers. Believers often call for prayer while they are attending public services.

The question arises as to whether or not the anointing

and prayer for the sick should be considered a sacrament of the church. We understand a sacrament to be a practice or ordinance commanded by the Lord, in which visible elements are used as a sign of the reception of a spiritual blessing. We believe the passage in the Book of James is divinely inspired and, as such, would seem to meet the conditions prescribed. Many Pentecostal churches practice the anointing of and prayer for the sick with more regularity than the Lord's Supper. There are now quite a number of churches of the older denominations that have stated times of prayer for the sick.

Prayer for the sick should always be accompanied by a time of heart-searching on the part of the sick person. Sickness is not always a direct result of sin, but there is such a possibility. "If he have committed sins," the apostle says. He also exhorts us to confess our sins to one another and pray for each other for healing. This is spiritually healthy.

Sickness is a curse. Healing is a blessing. I cannot remember having ever received great joy or blessing from taking a dose of medicine or a pill, but I have received tremendous joy and spiritual blessing from an instantaneous healing. To think that God is present, that He is real, that He has power today, and that He loves me enough to touch me personally and bring relief and healing brings floods of joy to my soul!

It may be well to note here that the Roman Catholic sacrament of Extreme Unction, which was a last rite used to prepare a soul for death, is now simply called "unction" and can be used to anoint the sick and pray for their recovery. This went into effect on January 1, 1974, according to Father Francis MacNutt.[3]

Healing, a Continuing Ministry of the Church

On many mission fields, praying for the sick in the regular services is an established practice. This brings more outsiders into the church to hear the gospel than perhaps any other feature of the services. It should always be stressed that the healing of the soul is first in importance. Try to get the seeker to accept Christ as his personal Saviour, and then pray for his illness.

I have personally seen many, many people come to the Lord in this manner. They come because some friend or neighbor has testified to them about a healing received or observed in the church. They want to be healed. They go to the church, hear the message of salvation, and accept Christ. They are prayed for and are healed. Then they go out and tell what Christ has done for them and others become interested. And the process is repeated. People are attracted to Christ because He meets all their needs. In fact, the Word says, "My God shall supply all your need according to his riches in glory by Christ Jesus" (Philippians 4:19). This certainly includes physical needs.

A healing service in the church should be conducted with great reverence. It is the power of God's Holy Spirit that heals. His presence should bring awe and reverence. Irreverence is bad at any time, and especially when we are invoking the power of God to bring relief and healing to an afflicted brother in Christ.

It is also important that the one who prays for the sick has compassion—empathy. Put yourself in the place of the one who comes to you for help. The One who is "the Healer" was "moved with compassion" for suffering humanity. If we are to do His work we should have the same compassionate spirit. It is when you are moved by their need that you will pray with intensity and fervor. Remember, it is the "fervent" prayer of a righteous man that avails.

It is important that those who have been healed be given an opportunity to witness in the church. It will prove a great blessing and inspiration to others to hear how God has answered prayers for some. This also strengthens the faith of the believers. It edifies, and that is Biblical! I have been in many revival campaigns where the crowds were so immense that it was impossible to pray for the people individually. Time was spent building up the people's faith in the Word of God. After a mass prayer (i.e., prayer for all the sick at the same time), the sick and afflicted were encouraged to accept their healing by faith. When they were sure that they were cured, they were permitted to come to the platform and testify. Sometimes the testimony service would last for an hour or more, each person speaking briefly. The "testimony line" is a lot more inspiring then the "healing line"!

If we really want to have a church that is known for its prayers for the sick and the results of those prayers, we need to be careful of our motives. Is it only that God may be exalted and His work extended? Or is there some personal ambition or desire for glory on our part? Sometimes it seems that what we are seeking is not the supernatural, but the spectacular. God has had to set aside many servants who have once been used to good advantage because unworthy motives entered in.

We must try to always keep things in their proper perspective. Apostles, prophets, and teachers are mentioned in the divine order before miracles and gifts of healings. (See 1 Corinthians 12:28.)

Some pastors have been known to sharply criticize members who have traveled long distances to get to some evangelist to be prayed for. If we preach the Word of God on healing and give prayer for the sick its due place in the church, there will be no need for the sick to go elsewhere. If we neglect our duties along this line, then those who need help are not to be blamed if they have to go afar to seek it.

A statement from Stanley Horton's book *Into All Truth* seems to be a fitting conclusion for this chapter:

We have seen from the Scriptures that it is unquestionably God's purpose and will to heal today. It is His promise; it is according to His nature; it is a part of the ministry of Christ; it is a part of the ministry of the Spirit; and it is a vital part of the continuing ministry of the church. It is linked so closely with salvation that to deny the possibility of healing is to deny the power of the present Saviour. It is linked so closely with missionary effort that to deny it is to lose one of the greatest means of advancing the cause of Christ in a suffering world. It is linked so closely with the spiritual life of the church that to deny it is to argue in behalf of a lifeless, formal organization taking the place of the living, Spirit-filled, Spirit-directed organism the church was meant to be.[4]

May God help His church to be what He intends it to be!

17

About Doctors and Medicines

The U.S. Department of Commerce indicates that the national income from medical and other health services for 1973 was over $41 billion.[1] This staggering sum certainly indicates that people want health and are seeking it. A great majority of those seeking health do so through physicians and medicines. It seems strange, in a way, that the Bible should be silent on these two subjects. The word *medicine*, with its plural, is mentioned only four times in the entire Bible. The word *physician*, with its plural, is mentioned only 12 times. On the other hand, there are scores of references to healing and health.

Does a person who believes in Jesus Christ as the Great Physician need the services of a medical doctor or medicines? What should be our attitude toward them? A clear understanding of this important subject should help us avoid radical extremes that have hindered the acceptance of the gospel of healing.

Once again we wish to call attention to the fact that God wants His children to be physically healthy. He wants us to "prosper and be in health" (3 John 2), as long as our souls also prosper. It will help us to keep in mind that our bodies are "programmed" for health and not for sickness. If a part of the body suffers some laceration, the proper elements rush to the affected part immediately to start the process of mending and healing. This is the way God made us, and it certainly indicates that He wants us to be well.

All thoughtful physicians will admit that the doctor himself cannot heal. No surgery or medicine can of itself bring healing. The surgeon or physician can take away defective parts, combat infection, fortify the physical systems, prescribe measures for health, but the body itself must cooperate or there will be no healing. As one doctor put it: "We bind the wounds . . . God heals."

If God wants us to be sound and healthy, then medical doctors who are doing their best to give us health and keep us healthy are cooperating with the will of God. We can deduce two things from this fact: (1) If physicians are doing God's will in trying to make us healthy, and are sincere and conscientious in their work, they can be a great blessing to humanity. (2) A Christian physician who is conscientious and sincere, and in touch with the Great Physician, can be an even greater blessing. We should appreciate these dedicated men and women, and not be critical of them.

There are some things God expects us to do for ourselves, and other things He alone can do. If you saw a worm on the back of your hand starting to burrow its way into your body, you would not call the church together to pray that the Lord would remove the worm! You would take immediate action and remove it yourself. The good Samaritan was commended by our Lord for applying the oil and wine and bandaging up the wounds of the man who had been beaten by robbers.

In God's message to the "shepherds of Israel" He accuses them of living off the flocks, and says also: "The diseased have ye not strengthened, neither have ye healed that which was sick, neither have ye bound up that which was broken" (Ezekiel 34:4). Christ, the Good Shepherd, is interested in the welfare of His flock, and His under-shepherds should follow His example.

Reasonable precautions and health measures should be taken by those who want to be at their best in God's service. Those who have studied physical health for years are usually in the best position to tell us what these precautions are.

Strict laws of sanitation were given to the Israelites when they were journeying toward the Promised Land.

They also had laws for the segregation of lepers long before health authorities recognized the need for such separation. The priests were in charge of inspecting the disease and imposing the quarantine. (See, for example, Leviticus 14, 15.)

Luke in his Gospel and the Acts of the Apostles gives us many accounts of miraculous healings in the ministry of the Lord, of Peter, and of Paul. He himself was called "the beloved physician" (Colossians 4:14), yet we have no record of his practicing medicine after he became a follower of Jesus Christ. He described the illness of the father of Publius, on the island of Malta, in medical terminology, but attributed his healing entirely to Paul's prayer. (See Acts 28:8, 9.)

Jesus Christ scathingly denounced religious hypocrisy, but we have no record of His ever condemning physicians or those who seek their help. He healed some who were not able to get their healing by these means. Luke gives us one such instance: "And a woman having an issue of blood twelve years, which had spent all her living upon physicians, neither could be healed of any, came behind him, and touched the border of his garment: and immediately her issue of blood stanched" (Luke 8:43, 44).

Although the Lord did not condemn physicians, He did not send anyone to them for help. He did not need to. He had, and still has, "all power in heaven and in earth." A study of the recorded healings of our Lord (there were many, many healings that were not recorded) will reveal that He healed many diseases and afflictions that would still be considered incurable.

Some believe that although the Lord healed physical ailments while He was here on earth, He now has given man the intelligence to combat these sicknesses and He rarely, if ever, intervenes directly in our day. They say we should use the "means" God has provided. We thank God for the development of the science of medicine which plays a large part in the relief of suffering humanity today. However, the "means" is not always a Godsend! If the diagnosis is wrong, the means may be harmful or even fatal.

Years ago my father worked for a drugstore in California. He found that medicine which helps the body combat one infirmity may weaken the body's resistance to another. As a result, those who continually use medicines become more and more dependent upon them. Some physicians are frank enough to admit that this is still true to a large extent today.

A Christian surgeon describes some of the problems of physicians as follows:

There continue to be new developments in the realm of disease which must be considered. As old diseases become curable by medical means, new strains develop.... As physical disease becomes more amenable to therapy, psychological and spiritual illness becomes more prevalent. The means of therapy alone produces its own group of diseases—so-called iatrogenic (doctor-produced) diseases. Some drugs may actually prevent health by producing an "unhealthy health," as by the abuse of tranquilizers. At times the search for the removal of abnormality may result in the cessation of the initial disease process by the substitution of a more serious problem than the first.[2]

By this we can see that the physicians themselves need our prayers as they continue to struggle against such odds.

We might well ask what is the purpose or objective of the medical profession? One physician is reported to have said at a convention of the American Medical Society, "I'm tired of producing healthy morons, healthy idiots, healthy criminals." We must recognize that man's illnesses are twofold—those of the body and those of the spirit. If we do not take care of man's spiritual needs, we are not helping society by making him healthy physically.

Psychoanalysis or psychiatry produces some strange and unexpected results when it shows that many adult "hang-ups" are the result of something that took place long ago in childhood. However, it is one thing to discover the origin or causative factor of our neuroses and quite another to rid ourselves of them. This is where spiritual help is needed. God can forgive and remove the sense of guilt and then fill our being with such joy and victory that we will be completely free from depression and fears. Medicine alone is not enough. The inner healing of the soul is most important to the outward health

God wants us to enjoy. The life of Christ within will impart well-being to every part of our body and soul. Many of the best writers on divine healing and health stress this very important truth.

Just as there are medical quacks, witch doctors, medicine men, and mediums who discredit the medical profession, there are also those who call themselves "ministers of the gospel" who have commercialized the gospel of healing and perverted its practice for personal fame or profit. An article by O. K. Armstrong published in the June 1971 issue of *Reader's Digest* sounds a warning against such. The title is "Beware the Commercialized Faith Healers."

Unfortunately, it is true that there have been and still are some who are unethical and even dishonest in their claims. This does not prove that the genuine does not exist. The very fact of a counterfeit would argue for a genuine. One who is genuinely used of God with a ministry of divine healing should never, under any circumstances, take glory for himself. He should always exalt Christ. Any gospel that does not exalt Jesus Christ is not divinely inspired. Christ, and not physical healing, should be the main theme of the preacher's message at all times. Paul saw many miracles of healing but he said, "We preach not ourselves, but Christ Jesus the Lord; and ourselves your servants for Jesus' sake" (2 Corinthians 4:5). Jesus Christ is the Healer. Would it not be dishonest to take pay for what someone else does? Captain Naaman fully expected to pay for his healing and went prepared to do so, but the prophet Elisha refused to receive payment for the miracle God had wrought.

In Acts 19 we read of special miracles that the Lord performed through the apostle Paul: "So that from his body were brought unto the sick handkerchiefs or aprons, and the diseases departed from them, and the evil spirits went out of them" (v. 12). This has been taken as a basis for using "anointed handkerchiefs." It seems that Paul was unable to go in person to see many of the sick who sought his help, and so he sent some personal effect, such as a handkerchief, to be placed upon the sick person as a point of contact, just as he would have laid hands upon him if he had been present. Elisha evidently believed in this sort of thing when he sent his servant with his own staff to place upon the son of the Shunammite woman (2 Kings 4:29). Whatever we may believe about it, it worked in Paul's case. Many testify today of having been healed in a similar manner. The pastor and the church pray over a handkerchief that they anoint with oil, and then it is conveyed to the sick person. Where there is sincere faith, definite healings occur.

This method has been greatly discredited by those who have "commercialized" its use. In some cases it has been carried so far as to become a sort of fetish or good luck charm that one purchases. This is very displeasing to the Lord and contrary to His gospel. He tells us that we have received freely and should give freely (Matthew 10:8). Peter told the lame man, "Such as I have *give* I thee" (Acts 3:6).

One of the few mentions of physicians in the Bible is in the case of King Asa. Here is the record: "Asa in the thirty and ninth year of his reign was diseased in his feet, until his disease was exceeding great: yet in his disease he sought not to the Lord, but to the physicians. And Asa slept with his fathers, and died in the one and fortieth year of his reign" (2 Chronicles 16:12, 13). Asa had been a good king and had served the Lord well, but toward the end of his reign a prophet rebuked him for making a military alliance with a heathen king. This made the king angry and he had the prophet thrown in jail. When he became very sick he no doubt was ashamed to seek God, after the way he had treated His prophet, so he went to the physicians instead. We do not know how competent the physicians were in his day. Some believe they were more like fetish priests or medicine men with very little true medical science. However that may be, the rebuke was not to the physicians but to Asa for turning away from the Lord. There is also an implication that he might have been healed had he put his case in the hands of the Lord.

Should a Bible-believing Christian take medicine? This question puzzles many sincere children of the Lord. Did Jesus use means to effect His cures? We read of His anointing with clay the eyes of a blind man, who then followed instructions and went to the pool, washed, and received his sight. In another case He used spittle on a deaf man, who also had an impediment of speech. (See John 9:6 and Mark 7:33). A fig poultice was placed upon the severe boil that was about to cause Hezekiah's death (2 Kings 20:7). Naaman was told to dip seven times in the river Jordan to be rid of his leprosy (2 Kings 5:14).

In none of these cases is it stated or even suggested that the means prescribed had any curative properties. It seems they were simply symbolic and used as a test of entire obedience to the Word of the Lord. In every case it was the power of God that brought healing.

Does this mean that the sick should give up his medicine after he has been prayed for? A word of caution must be sounded here lest any take an extreme course which could lead to a more serious condition.

Whether you should take medicine or not depends on whether you are well or sick after you have been prayed for. Certainly the decision to discontinue taking medicine for some sickness should not be based on presumption or the advice of a well-meaning friend. The decision should be based on the facts of the situation.

Should the one who has been healed return to the physician for examination? Jesus did not condemn the human diagnosticians of his day. He sent the 10 lepers to the priests after they had asked Him for mercy: "And when he saw them, he said unto them, Go show yourselves unto the priests" (Luke 17:14).

Some today, in their desire to exercise faith, make the mistake of saying they are healed when in fact they are not. This is not faith but presumption. A statement adopted by the Assemblies of God General Presbytery points out that those healed in the Bible did not testify to divine healing until the healing was actually accomplished by divine power.

In any case, it should be the sick person himself who decides whether he will give up his medicine or not. If you tell him to do so you can be accused of practicing medicine without a license.

The testimony of A. B. Simpson on this matter is given in the following quotation:

I have not found any serious practical difficulty in dealing with the question of remedies. . . . There is no use in giving up remedies without a real personal faith in Christ. And where one really commits his case to Christ and believes that He has undertaken it, he does not want, as a rule, to have any other hand touch it, or indeed see that anything else is necessary. Where persons have real faith in Christ's supernatural help they will not want remedies.[3]

This is the testimony of one who had been dependent upon remedies for 20 years and then became so filled with the life of Christ that he found the remedies unnecessary.

Civil laws may make it necessary at times to call for medical assistance for members of our family. In such cases we are to remember that the Bible tells us to obey the laws. This should not be because of a lack of faith, but to comply with such laws and set a good example as a Christian. Sometimes we would gladly trust the Lord for ourselves, but our children may not have the same faith and may resent a forcing (as they see it) of our beliefs on them. After raising our own five children on the foreign mission field and seeing God heal them time after time, I am glad to report that all of them have a strong faith in the Lord as their Healer.

Here I might insert a word about medical missionaries. These dedicated men and women have done much to break down prejudice and create a favorable attitude toward the gospel. Many people have been won to Christ through consecrated missionary doctors and nurses. It might also be added that the lives of many missionaries have been saved because of missionary hospitals and doctors.

However, we need to face the facts squarely, and in doing so we will see that in many cases the response to the gospel has been very small in comparison to the investment made in terms of men and money. When a missionary doctor is able to restore to health one who has been desperately sick, the person is apt to think, "The foreigner's medicine is powerful!" When a person who is equally sick is restored to health through fervent prayer and faith, the healed person thinks, "The foreigner's God is powerful!" Which of the two results is more in line with our objectives?

Earthly physicians and remedies may be good, but the Great Physician, the One who made us in the first place, is far superior. He is a specialist in every disease. He is always present to help when we need Him. He has power to actually heal and not just help the healing processes of the body. There is nothing that He cannot do!

18
By Their Fruits

Those who question the value of the doctrine of divine healing would do well to use the Lord's own test. He said, "By their fruits ye shall know them"(Matthew 7:20). Although you may never have seen an orange tree, if you see a tree with oranges growing all over it you immediately know what kind of a tree it is. Even a child can tell a tree by its fruits.

What are the fruits of prayer for the sick? We present the following facts for your careful consideration.

Results of the Healing Ministry of Christ

(1) *It showed God's approval.* John the Baptist was a widely acknowledged prophet of God. Jesus spoke very highly of him. John had borne witness that Jesus was the Son of God (John 1:34). This was a valuable testimony. But Jesus said, "I have greater witness than that of John: for the works which the Father hath given me to finish, the same works that I do, bear witness of me, that the Father hath sent me" (John 5:36). Peter told the multitude he addressed on the Day of Pentecost that Jesus of Nazareth was "a man approved of God among you by miracles and wonders and signs, which God did by him in the midst of you, as ye yourselves also know" (Acts 2:22).

(2) *It convinced the people that He was God-sent.* Nicodemus, a Pharisee and a ruler of the Jews, told Jesus, "Rabbi, we know that thou art a teacher come from God: for no man can do these miracles that thou doest, except God be with him" (John 3:2). After Lazarus had been

raised from the dead, those who opposed Christ con-ferred together and said, "What do we? for this man doeth many miracles. If we let him thus alone, all men will believe on him" (John 11:47, 48). Even his enemies ad-mitted that Christ's miracles would convince the people that He was the Messiah.

(3) *It caused multitudes to follow Him.* "And a great multitude followed him, because they saw his miracles which he did on them that were diseased" (John 6:2). "When Jesus had finished these sayings, he departed from Galilee, and came into the coasts of Judea beyond Jordan; and great multitudes followed him; and he healed them there" (Matthew 19:1, 2). Jesus healed a leper and told him to say nothing about it, "But he went out, and began to publish it much, and to blaze abroad the matter, in-somuch that Jesus could no more openly enter into the city, but was without in desert places: and they came to him from every quarter" (Mark 1:45). When the power of the Lord is working in your meetings, you don't have to have an ideal location!

(4) *It caused people to glorify God.* "Insomuch that the multitude wondered, when they saw the dumb to speak, the maimed to be whole, the lame to walk, and the blind to see: and they glorified the God of Israel" (Matthew 15:31). Jesus told a paralytic man that was brought to him for healing that his sins were forgiven. After this he told him to get up, take up his bed, and go home. "And im-mediately he arose, took up the bed, and went forth be-fore them all; insomuch that they were all amazed, and glorified God, saying, We never saw it on this fashion" (Mark 2:12).

Results of the Healing Ministry of the Apostles

(1) *It showed God's approval.* In the Great Commission Jesus had told his disciples to go preach the gospel to every creature. He said that certain signs would follow those who believe. Among other things, He promised that they would lay hands on the sick and the sick would be healed. (See Mark 16:15-18.) What happened? "They went forth, and preached every where, the Lord working with them, and confirming the word with signs following.

Amen" (Mark 16:20). The ability to see these signs done in the name of Jesus showed His approval on their ministry. Speaking of our great salvation, the author of the Epistle to the Hebrews says that it was first spoken of by the Lord, "and was confirmed unto us by them that heard him; God also bearing them witness, both with signs and wonders, and with divers miracles, and gifts of the Holy Ghost" (Hebrews 2:3, 4). Wouldn't you like to have God bear witness to your ministry? This is the way He does it. There could be nothing more convincing!

(2) *It convinced the people.* The Jewish rulers, elders, and scribes were quite perturbed about the healing of the crippled man who for years had sat by the gate of the temple begging. They counseled together and said, "What shall we do to these men? for that indeed a notable miracle hath been done by them is manifest to all them that dwell in Jerusalem; and we cannot deny it" (Acts 4:16). These were perpetuators of a religion and not seekers after truth. They could not deny the facts of the case, but did not want to change from the traditional beliefs of their fathers! The miracle of the healing of the man of Lystra who had been crippled since birth was so convincing that the pagan people said: "The gods are come down to us in the likeness of men" (Acts 14:11).

(3) *It caused multitudes to receive the gospel.* There were three supernatural signs on the Day of Pentecost. People were so convinced by what they saw and heard that Peter needed only to give an explanation of what was happening and tell them how to receive Christ as their Saviour. "Then they that gladly received his word were baptized: and the same day there were added unto them about three thousand souls" (Acts 2:41). (Note: Healing was not the supernatural sign used by the Lord in this case. However, the principle is still valid that it was the supernatural that caused this great crowd to turn to Christ and accept Him.)

After the healing of the crippled beggar we are told: "Many of them which heard the word believed; and the number of the men was about five thousand" (Acts 4:4). Pastor, how would you like to have 5,000 men in your congregation? The signs continued, "And by the hands of the apostles were many signs and wonders wrought among the people" (Acts 5:12). "There came also a multitude out of the cities round about unto Jerusalem, bringing sick folks, and them which were vexed with unclean spirits: and they were healed every one" (v. 16).

(4) *It caused God to be glorified.* When the lame man was healed, he leaped and walked and praised God. "And all the people saw him walking and praising God" (Acts 3:9). In Ephesus God did special miracles through the apostle Paul. Some "vagabond Jews" attempted to imitate Paul and cast out demons. They were overpowered by the demons and fled "naked and wounded. And this was known to all the Jews and Greeks also dwelling at Ephesus; and fear fell on them all, and the name of the Lord Jesus was magnified" (Acts 19:16, 17). Doctrines of demons do not glorify the Lord Jesus Christ.

The two cases in Acts 9—the healing of Aeneas and the raising of Dorcas—have already been mentioned, but do not forget the results of these two miracles of healing. In the case of Aeneas we are told: "And all that dwelt at Lydda and Sharon saw him, and turned to the Lord" (v. 35). The raising of Dorcas "was known throughout all Joppa; and many believed in the Lord" (v. 42). Who can deny that this was good fruit?

Results of the Healing Ministry in Our Day

If the healing ministry of Christ and of His followers showed God's approval, convinced the people, attracted multitudes, and glorified God, then we should expect to see the same results from the healing ministry of sincere Christians today. Let us examine some of the well-verified examples of both personal healings and evangelistic campaigns where prayer was offered for the sick. Obviously, we will have room for only a few of the many, many accounts available, so we will choose some that have been very well documented or with which we are personally acquainted.

Wesley R. Steelberg was 6 years old when he was stricken with spinal meningitis. He had triple curvature of the spine and his head touched his heels backward. Brain fever and other complications turned him into a hopeless spastic. The attending physician gave no hopes that he would live, but said his brain would be so charred by the fever that he would be a gruesome, hopeless imbecile if he lived. Some people who went to see him turned sick at the sight.

The Steelbergs were good Methodists, and were living in Denver, Colorado. They heard about prayer for the sick and invited a pastor to come and pray for their boy. The pastor came, but turned sick when he saw the child. He felt that his prayer had gotten nowhere. Later while riding his bicycle home from work, the father heard a voice saying, "Submit yourselves, therefore, to God. Resist the devil and he will flee from you." He believed, went into the room, and he and his wife prayed for the child. They felt no movement, yet the body was straightened out completely. The boy slept for 20 hours and awoke perfectly well.

Brother Steelberg started preaching when he was 17. He pastored a number of large churches, was a well-known youth leader, and became a well-loved general superintendent of the Assemblies of God. His biography *All for Jesus* gives further details of his healing and his remarkably fruitful ministry in the work of the Lord.

J. P. Wannenmacher was born in Hungary. His mother died of tuberculosis and a sister died of the same disease at the age of 14. He began to suffer from tuberculosis of the bone. They lived in a health resort, but the fine physicians there could not help him.

The family moved to America when he was 14. He had two more operations and the physicians recommended the amputation of his foot. Hundreds of dollars were spent for "treatments" by Christian Science practitioners to no avail. In desperation Wannenmacher began to seek God, but didn't know how to find Him. He was told of a church where they prayed for the sick. At this church he heard that Christ is our Saviour and Healer. He accepted the good news and was saved and instantly healed.

He says, "To the glory of God, I can say that since that time, 55 years ago, I have been privileged to be active in the service of the Lord as a messenger of the glorious Gospel." Brother Wannenmacher was the pastor of a large church in Milwaukee, Wisconsin, for many years and also, as an accomplished musician, has blessed thousands with his violin music.

Nicky Cruz is a well-publicized example of how God can deliver from drug addiction and heal all the hurts and hates of the inner man. Born in Puerto Rico of parents who practiced spiritism and witchcraft, he once heard his own mother say that he was not her child but the child of the devil. He began to hate her and everyone else. In New York he was "running wild on a one-way street to the electric chair." The leader of a much-feared gang, the "Mau Maus," he was bound by drugs and in constant trouble with the law and with his fellowman in general.

Through the ministry of David Wilkerson he was brought to the Lord, delivered from his old life, and made a new creature in Christ. His story, which is told in a fascinating manner in the best-seller *Run Baby Run*,[1] is introduced by Billy Graham and then has a foreword by Professor Edward D. O'Connor of the University of Notre Dame. Prof. O'Connor has this to say:

Nicky's story is possibly the most dramatic in the history of the Pentecostal movement, but it is not unique. Nicky is only a very colorful representative of a vast number of people who, in the past few decades, have been delivered from crime, alcoholism, drug addiction, prostitution, homosexuality, and almost every type of perversion and degeneration known to man. Psychiatric care, medical treatment, and spiritual counseling had failed to affect these people, when with astounding abruptness they were set free from their bonds by the power of the Holy Spirit and led to a life of useful service and sometimes of profound prayer.[2]

The Teen Challenge centers and coffee houses which have been set up all over the U.S. and in many cities in Europe give ample proof that God can and does completely take away drug addiction when all other efforts fail. Many times the victim is instantly delivered without withdrawal pains. Usually, he is then sent to a Teen Challenge rehabilitation center where he is further grounded in the faith and instructed in the Christian life.

The percentage of complete cures through this program of prayer and faith has caused men like Art Linkletter and medical authorities of the military to say that Teen Challenge is more effective than any other program now known in delivering people from drugs. Since drug addiction (and the crime involved by those who are "hooked" trying to support their habit, which may run up to $100 or more per day) is one of the number one problems here in the U.S., we should certainly welcome this form of the healing power of Christ as the solution.

Salvation-healing Campaigns have been mightily used of God for the extension of His kingdom in many parts of the world. We have already pointed out that some have "commercialized" this method and done great harm to the cause of Christ. This should not make us lose sight of the fact that such campaigns are a valid and very effective means of carrying out the Great Commission. Let us look at a few cases that I am well acquainted with.

In January 1956, the missionary-evangelist Richard Jeffery began a campaign in San Salvador, the capital of El Salvador, Central America. God blessed, the city was stirred, many miracles of healing took place, and opposition set in. The evangelist was accused of practicing medicine without a license and had to go to court. During the time he was waiting for the trial he was not forbidden to continue preaching, and so the campaign which was originally planned for about 3 weeks lasted for 3 months and 5 days! This proved to be a real blessing, because it gave time to stabilize the work.

He was not convicted by the court, but when his 3-month permit expired the authorities refused to renew it and he had to leave the country. Twenty-six chartered buses of people accompanied the evangelist and his family to the Guatemalan border where a farewell service was conducted. What were the results of this campaign and the dedicated efforts of those who carried out the follow-up?

In 1956 the Assemblies of God had one church in San Salvador with 16 members, a Sunday school with 100 in attendance, and no branch Sunday schools. In 1960 there were 20 Assemblies of God churches in the city, 1,200 church members, 7,700 people attending Sunday school in the main churches, and 155 branch Sunday schools. The work has continued to grow and expand. This would not have happened if it had not been for the outstanding miracles (paralytics healed, sight restored to some who were blind, many deaf healed, and various kinds of sicknesses healed) that attracted the multitudes, convinced the people of the power of the gospel, and caused them to turn to Christ.

Holguin, Cuba, is an example of the great revival that swept many cities of Cuba in a similar fashion in 1950 and 1951. Missionary James Nicholson and I were the evangelists in this campaign. The city offered to let us use the city park free of charge with even the electricity furnished. Two radio stations gave time for daily broadcasts and prayer for the sick. We had a radio broadcast at 10 o'clock in the morning, another at noon, an evangelistic service at 2 o'clock in the afternoon in the city park, and another in the evening at 7:30. Reports from similar campaigns in other cities had already stirred this community, and we had about 9,000 people in attendance the first night.

Many healings and some outstanding miracles took place. There were usually from 4,000 to 5,000 people in attendance at the afternoon services (standing in the hot sun), and about 10,000 to 12,000 in the evening services. The people responded eagerly when asked if they wanted a church in their city where they could be prayed for at any time. In less than 3 weeks we received nearly $5,000 for the purchase of what had been a shoe factory. It would hold about 700 people. The campaign closed one Sunday night, and the next Sunday they were able to start worshiping in their own building.

One year later my wife and I visited the church in Holguin. At that time they had an average Sunday School attendance in their main church of over 400, and had established about 30 branch Sunday schools. They were reaching over 2,000 people each week with the Word of God in this manner. Later these Sunday schools developed and many became outstations or sovereign local assemblies. Many young people from that church went to Bible school and became pastors and evangelists.

In a number of important cities of Cuba a strong church was established as the result of a single revival campaign. These congregations built their own church buildings and became entirely self-supporting. They also opened branch churches in the areas around them. In every case of an outstanding revival, divine healing played an important role. Some of the largest campaigns were held in Santiago de Cuba, Camaguey, Ciego de Avila, Holguin, Banes, Victoria de las Tunas, Guantanamo, and Baracoa. In each of these places a good church was established. It seems to me that we cannot improve on Christ's method of teaching, preaching, and healing.

Other Fruits

Other fruits of salvation-healing campaigns were very evident. *The circulation of the Word of God* was a direct result of the literal interpretation and strong emphasis placed on the Bible. An article in the Bible Society Record of July 1952, written by the society's secretary for the West Indies, Dr. J. Gonzalez Molina, had as its title "We Could Have Used 100,000 Testaments." There was a picture of part of the crowd of some 20,000 attending the Camaguey campaign, and he reported that 3,500 Bibles, 10,000 New Testaments, and 25,000 Gospel portions were sold in this one campaign. The entire stock of the Bible Society was exhausted by the extraordinary hunger for the Word of God.

Missionary Sterling Stewart reported that 1,200 Bibles, 4,500 New Testaments, and 40,000 Gospel portions were sold in the campaign in San Salvador. Similar results were reported in most of the campaigns. Any lover of the Bible, the Word of God, will surely agree that this is a good fruit!

Publicity for the gospel which would have cost thousands of dollars and still not have been nearly so effective, was given by radio and by the press because of the extraordinary nature of the events and the vast crowds that attended. In this way the power of the gospel was made known to tens of thousands of people who might not have been reached with the gospel by any other means of communication.

All classes are reached in this type of evangelistic campaign. Since all are interested in health, and since the medical profession does not have the answer in so many cases, people from all walks of life want to find healing and health. They not only attend the campaign, but many professional men and women are healed and converted and become a great help in establishing the local church.

Self-support of the local church is usually achieved as soon as it is established, since there is a sufficient number of converts to begin with. This, of course, means there is no strain on the missionary budget and no limit to the possible expansion of the work. The "indigenous principle" (self-support, self-government, and self-propagation) was Paul's missionary method. It should be ours as well. It is quite possible in the manner just described.

Open doors for the gospel result from this type of campaign. We have seen many cases where the mayor of a town, perhaps with some other municipal officials, would bring or send a special request to have a campaign in their town. I remember one case where a petition was received asking for a campaign. It was signed by over 500 people. What an opportunity! In one country of West Africa a remarkable campaign with many miracles of healing was held in the capital city. The president of the country then asked the evangelist to hold a campaign in a second city, and paid all the expenses! This happened in 1973.

Rapid evangelization of an entire nation is possible through this God-given means. Since it seems evident that the coming of the Lord is very near, we must not neglect the means that is perhaps the most effective of all for getting the gospel to every creature and fulfilling His last command!

19

The Role of the Holy Spirit in Healing

The need for physical healing in the world is very evident in view of the fact that in 1971 the American people (U.S.A.) spent $51.4 billion for medical care.[1] In recent years there has been a great resurgence of interest in divine healing, partly due to the many published testimonies of miraculous cures in answer to prayer. However, in searching for the power or process that will make this healing become operative, the role of the Holy Spirit is often overlooked.

The Promise of the Holy Spirit

First, we should recognize that Christ told His followers it was better for them that He should go away, so the Holy Spirit could come. He promised that He would send the Spirit, and that they would be able to continue His work on earth, doing even greater things than He had done (John 16:7; 14:12). They were told not to leave Jerusalem for their preaching ministry until they had received "power from on high" (Luke 24:49). The word translated "power" here is *dunamis* which implies special miraculous power or a miracle itself. They were to receive spiritual power, supernatural power, to do a spiritual work. How was this power to be given? Just before His ascension Jesus told His followers: "Ye shall receive power, after that the Holy Ghost is come upon you: and ye shall be witnesses unto me both in Jerusalem, and in all Judea, and in Samaria, and unto the uttermost part of the earth" (Acts 1:8).

The promised Spirit descended on the Day of Pentecost. The followers of the Lord did receive supernatural power, and began their supernatural ministry in the power of the Holy Spirit.

It is interesting to note that when Christ promised to send His followers "another Comforter" the words *allos Parakletos* were used. We know that *paraclete* means "one called to one's side to help or give aid." The word *allos* is significant because it means "another of the same sort."[2] Christ was sending the Spirit to take His place. Since the Spirit was like Him, He could be expected to carry on the same type of work Jesus had done. If far more than half of Jesus' time was used in ministry to the sick, certainly the Holy Spirit would continue His work.

We are told in Acts 10:38 that "God anointed Jesus of Nazareth with the Holy Ghost and with power: who went about doing good, and healing all that were oppressed of the devil; for God was with Him." This anointing took place at the beginning of Christ's public ministry. He said: "The Spirit of the Lord is upon me, because he hath anointed me to preach the gospel to the poor; he hath sent me to heal the brokenhearted, to preach deliverance to the captives, and recovering of sight to the blind, to set at liberty them that are bruised" (Luke 4:18). Physical healing through the power of the Holy Spirit was an important result of the anointing mentioned here.

Some may ask, "Why did Jesus have to be anointed with the Holy Spirit, since He himself was divine?" The eminent English clergyman and author F. B. Meyer answers, "Because His human nature needed to be empowered by the Spirit, before even He could do successful service in this world. . . . Never forget that our Lord's ministry was not in the power of the second person of the blessed Trinity, but in the power of the third person."[3] It seems that in His earthly ministry Jesus did not want to use power that would not be available to His followers; so He did His healings and miracles through the power of the Holy Spirit, a power that is available to believers today.

We know that Jesus Christ has been exalted and is now at the right hand of the Father. How does His supernatural work of saving and healing continue today? We read in 2 Corinthians 3:17, 18 (ASV): "Now the Lord is the Spirit: and where the Spirit of the Lord is, there is liberty. But we all, with unveiled face beholding as in a mirror the glory of the Lord, are transformed into the same image from glory to glory, even as from the Lord the Spirit."

Christ is now here working in and with His church in the person of the Holy Spirit—the same Holy Spirit that anointed Him and enabled Him to do the mighty works recorded in the Gospels. This same Spirit enabled Peter, Paul, Stephen, Philip, and others to do mighty miracles. "The Lord the Spirit" is still active today and is doing the same type of work He has always done.

The Spirit's Quickening Power

Another key verse on the nature of the work of the Holy Spirit is found in Romans 8:11: "But if the Spirit of him that raised up Jesus from the dead dwelleth in you, he that raised up Christ Jesus from the dead shall give life also to your mortal bodies through his Spirit that dwelleth in you" (ASV). The marginal reading is "because of his Spirit that dwelleth in you." It seems to me that far too many Bible interpreters and teachers think that this verse refers only to the resurrection. Since they believe it refers to a future time, the present-day work of the Holy Spirit—giving more life to our physical bodies—is ignored, and its blessings are lost. Let us look again at the text.

The Interlinear Literal Translation of the Greek New Testament gives the passage as follows: "But if the Spirit of him who raised up Jesus from among [the] dead dwells in you, he who raised up the Christ from among [the] dead will quicken also your mortal bodies on account of his Spirit that dwells in you."[4] *Strong's Concordance* gives the meaning of "quicken" as: "to (re-)vitalize (lit. or fig.): make alive, give life."[5] Notice that the reference is to our "mortal" or physical bodies. The promise is that the Holy Spirit will "revitalize," "give life to," or accelerate the life processes of our physical bodies. There can be no doubt that the Holy Spirit is capable of doing this. It was the Holy Spirit that overshadowed the Virgin Mary and gave physical life to our Lord Jesus Christ (Luke 1:35). It was through the power of the Holy Spirit that Christ healed the sick (Acts 10:38). And it was the power of the Holy Spirit that resurrected our Lord (Romans 8:11).

If the power of the Spirit is sufficient to produce life in the first place and to restore life to a dead person, certainly it must be sufficient to heal the sick.

Notice also that it is our *mortal body* that is to be revitalized. This is the earthly body, the natural body, which is to be replaced by a spiritual body at the resurrection. The mortal body will be changed, or exchanged, and the victorious believers in Christ will be clothed with immortality. (See 1 Corinthians 15:40-54.)

The Indwelling Spirit

Another clue to the present-day application of our text is the fact that the revitalization, the impartation of more life, is the result of the Spirit residing within the believer. Surely the Holy Spirit is not residing in dead bodies that are waiting for the resurrection! With the life-giving power of the Holy Spirit dwelling within the Christian, why shouldn't he enjoy vibrant, radiant spiritual and physical health?

Jesus said that the Spirit had anointed Him for the purpose of healing the brokenhearted (Luke 4:18). There is much sadness in the world today, and physicians, generally speaking, can do little or nothing to help individuals with crushed spirits. The sadness itself may produce illness or take away the will to live which is so important to recovery. Jesus is the physician who can heal the whole man. He starts on the inside and changes the sadness and misery to "joy unspeakable and full of glory." How does He do it? He has sent the Comforter to abide with us forever (John 14:16). He comforts us in our sorrows and griefs. He produces in us the fruits of love, joy, and peace. There is no reason for a Spirit-filled Christian to suffer from psychosomatic illnesses, depression, or neuroses. We need only to surrender to God's will and allow the Holy Spirit the full occupancy of His temple—our bodies.

It was the power of the Holy Spirit that worked through the apostle Paul and caused his ministry to be so successful. He wrote to the believers in Rome: "I dare not judge how effectively he has used others, but I know this: He has used me to win the Gentiles to God. I have won them by my message and by the good way I have lived before them, and by miracles done through me as signs from God—all by the Holy Spirit's power" (Romans 15:18, 19, *Living Bible*). Power to live for God, power to preach, and power for the healing of the sick are available through the Holy Spirit.

It should not be thought strange that the Holy Spirit would have power to do miracles and perform wonderful healings, because it is the Holy Spirit himself that gives the supernatural gifts of healing, of miracles, and of faith (1 Corinthians 12:1-11). Let us not overlook the significance of this fact. Practically all the pastors and evangelists who have been signally used of God in praying for the sick have been filled with the Holy Spirit.

George Jeffreys tell us that Evan Roberts, who was so mightily used of God in the great Welch Revival, suffered from severe weakness and other ailments, but the moment he received the Holy Spirit all this disappeared and did not return. He gives his own testimony also, telling how he suffered as a youth from a facial paralysis that began to go down one side of his body. The Spirit of the Lord came upon him in such power that it felt like his head was connected to a powerful electric battery. He was quickened from head to foot by the Holy Spirit and was completely healed.[6]

The great preaching and healing ministry of Smith Wigglesworth began when he was filled with the Holy Spirit. There are numerous testimonies of this nature. It appears quite evident that the miraculous powers which are so needed for the execution of the task God has given us must be received as a result of being filled with the Holy Spirit. Wigglesworth says, "We have been seeing wonderful miracles these last days and they are only a little of what we are going to see. I believe that we are right on the threshold of wonderful things, but I want to emphasize that all these things will be through the power of the Holy Spirit."[7]

Jesus promised that supernatural signs would follow the ministry of those who believed in Him (Mark 16:17, 18). The Bible tells us that this did happen: "And they went forth, and preached every where, the Lord working with them, and confirming the word with signs following" (v.20). The same thought is brought out in Hebrews 2:3, 4. Moffatt translates verse 4 as follows: "While God corroborated their testimony with signs and wonders and a variety of miraculous powers, distributing the Holy Spirit as it pleased him." Other Scripture passages that we have already examined show the Holy Spirit to be the Source of the convincing, miracle-working power that extended the gospel of Christ to practically all the known world in 1 century.

Healings through the ministry of the early preachers of the gospel brought glory to Christ. Christ said the Holy Spirit would glorify Him, and this is one way He does it. Stephen was "full of faith and of the Holy Ghost" (Acts 6:5), and he "did great wonders and miracles among the people" (v. 8). We, too, can be full of the Holy Spirit and bring glory to Christ through the healings and miracles that accompany our ministry.

The followers of the Lord were sent forth to heal the sick, body and soul. They were told where the power was to come from. They tarried until they received this power, and their preaching was accompanied with "signs following." If we expect to follow Biblical methods and get Biblical results, let us obey the Biblical injunction and keep on being filled with the Spirit (Ephesians 5:18). Then, when we minister, we can confidently expect the power of the Lord to be present to heal (Luke 5:17).

May the Holy Spirit who guides into all truth lead us into a full revelation of this great truth which, though it is widely neglected, is so needed in the world today.

He sent his word, and healed them. Psalm 107:20

20

Healing Through the Word

In considering the dynamics of divine healing we have studied the gifts of the Spirit that are directly related to healing and the role of the Holy Spirit in healing. Let us now look at another very important factor—the Word of God.

Although the Bible is available in more translations than ever before and enjoying its greatest circulation, comparatively few people seem to realize its limitless power. As a man is, so is his word. As God is, so is His Word. God's Word is as dependable as He is. To doubt His Word is to doubt Him. Note well the following facts about God's Word.

God's Word Is the Highest Authority

The word of an absolute monarch or dictator can mean life or death to his subjects. However, the power or authority of his word is limited by the extent of his domain. Our God is King of kings and Lord of lords. There is no limitation of His domain. All things were created by and for Him. All things must obey Him. Jesus Christ said: "All power [authority] is given unto me in heaven and in earth" (Matthew 28:18). Those who heard Him in Capernaum "were astonished at his doctrine: for his word was with power" (Luke 4:32). He was able to speak to the winds and the sea (Matthew 8:26, 27); to trees (Mark 11:14); to demons (Matthew 8:32; 17:18); and to the sick and afflicted commanding healing and health, and both

156

the forces of nature and the powers of darkness had to obey His Word. There is no higher authority. When He orders a thing it is final.

God's Word Is the Greatest Power

People are continually seeking new and greater sources of power: energy-producing power, social and political power, power to persuade, power to destroy, psychic powers, and so on. However, in all their searching the greatest power in the universe is often overlooked or ignored. Look at the power of God's Word.

God's Word has creative power. In the Genesis account of Creation we find that God simply said, "Let there be light," and there was light. All through the 6 days of Creation the same procedure was used. He simply spoke the word and things came to pass. The Psalmist tells us: "By the word of the Lord were the heavens made; and all the hosts of them by the breath of his mouth. For he spake, and it was done; he commanded, and it stood fast" (Psalm 33:6, 9). In Hebrews 11:3 we read: "Through faith we understand that the worlds were framed by the word of God, so that things which are seen were not made of things which do appear." When related to healing this means that the God who created man in the first place can repair his body, regardless of the difficulty, and even supply new parts if necessary!

God's Word has regenerative power. The apostle Peter states that we are "born again, not of corruptible seed, but of incorruptible, by the word of God, which liveth and abideth for ever" (1 Peter 1:23). He also tells us that it is through the precious promises of the Word that we are made "partakers of the divine nature" (2 Peter 1:4). The more we can partake of the divine nature the more we will be free from the turmoil, worries, and inner conflicts that produce ill health. Being filled with the divine nature we will love the Lord with all our heart and our neighbor as ourself. We cannot imagine Jesus being unable to do His Father's work because of sickness or ill health. Neither should we as sons of God, partakers of His nature, doing His will, be hindered by physical illness. The regenerative power of the Word of God can cleanse and heal all the inner recesses of our being.

God's Word Has Healing Power

The 107th Psalm tells of people being afflicted and drawing near the gates of death. Then they cry to the Lord and He delivers them. We are told how in verse 20, "He sent his word, and healed them, and delivered them from their destructions." The Roman centurion who came to Jesus seeking healing for his paralytic servant recognized the power of Jesus' Word. He said: "Lord, I am not worthy that thou shouldest come under my roof: but speak the word only, and my servant shall be healed" (Matthew 8:8). Note that this officer believed in the authority of Jesus, so much so that he believed the spoken word would be as powerful as the physical presence of Christ! Jesus highly commended him for his faith, then spoke the word and his servant was healed that very hour. Many believe that they would have faith to be healed if they could see Jesus standing by their side. We have His Word. That is all that is necessary. Over and over Jesus simply spoke the word and people were healed and delivered from all kinds of maladies and sicknesses. There is power, healing power, in the Word of God.

God's Word Is Completely Reliable

Truth is an outstanding characteristic of our God. Balaam the prophet said: "God is not a man, that he should lie; neither the son of man, that he should repent: hath he said, and shall he not do it? Or hath he spoken, and shall he not make it good?" (Numbers 23:19). God made some wonderful promises to the Israelites when He brought them out of their 400-year period of slavery. Did He keep the promises? Look at Joshua 21:45: "There failed not aught of any good thing which the Lord had spoken unto the house of Israel; all came to pass." At the end of Solomon's prayer of dedication of the temple, he exclaimed: "Blessed be the Lord, that hath given rest unto his people Israel, according to all that he promised: there hath not failed one word of all his good promise, which he promised by the hand of Moses his servant"

(1 Kings 8:56). Remember: God always keeps His Word.

Some people make promises and then change their minds and decide not to do what they offered. God tells us: "I am the Lord, I change not; therefore ye sons of Jacob are not consumed" (Malachi 3:6). James tells us that in Him there "is no variableness, neither shadow of turning" (James 1:17). Perhaps a clearer translation is as follows: " . . . the Father of lights, with whom can be no variation, neither shadow that is cast by turning" (ASV). He does not change His mind. He can be counted on at all times to keep whatever He promises.

There are others that make a promise in all good faith and then find that circumstances make it impossible for them to fulfill their promise. What a comfort to know that with God nothing is impossible. He always has the ability to do what He offers. You can utterly depend upon all His promises. Among those promises, remember, is the covenant and ordinance that He made with his people to be their Physician. (See Exodus 15:25, 26.)

God's Word Is Eternal

His promises are not subject to the limitations of time. He lives forever. Since He is perfect in wisdom and understanding, He makes no mistakes. His promises do not have to be revised and updated from time to time. The Psalmist says: "For ever, O Lord, thy word is settled in heaven. Thy faithfulness is unto all generations" (Psalm 119:89, 90). Jesus said: "Heaven and earth shall pass away, but my words shall not pass away" (Matthew 24:35). Isaiah the prophet says: "The grass withereth, the flower fadeth: but the word of our God shall stand for ever" (Isaiah 40:8). Surely this should let us know that the One who revealed himself as the Healer of His people still heals today. The One who "sent his word, and healed" in the day of the Psalmist, will send that same Word and heal us today. Christ's word to the leper, "Be thou clean," can be applied to those of us who live in the 20th century as well as to those of the first.

Jesus Christ Is the Living Word

Why is He called the *Word?* A word is simply a vehicle to convey a thought or an idea. No language and no rhetoric could so eloquently convey to us the idea of God's love toward a lost humanity as the life and death of His only begotten Son. He is the "Logos" of God. He is the Word that was with God in the beginning of Creation, and by Him were all things created (John 1:1-3). "In him was life; and the life was the light of men" (John 1:4). He said, "I am . . . the life" (John 14:6; 11:25). He also came to bring us life more abundant (John 10:10). If we want the blessing of healing and health we should seek the Healer himself, the Source of life. As the life of Christ, that life that destroys everything produced by evil and energizes us by His Spirit, penetrates every part of our being healing, health, and happiness will be the inevitable result.

The Word of God Has Life

Although this may seem like a strange or mysterious statement, let us examine the evidence. In the Epistle to the Hebrews we read: "For the word of God is living, and active, and sharper than any two-edged sword, and piercing even to the dividing of soul and spirit, of both joints and marrow, and quick to discern the thoughts and intents of the heart" (Hebrews 4:12, ASV). How can an inanimate object do these things? Christ himself declared, "The words that I speak unto you, they are spirit, and they are life" (John 6:63). Summing up the great revival in Ephesus the key factor is given thus, "So mightily grew the word of God and prevailed" (Acts 19:20).

The Word of God produces life. We are born from above through the Word (1 Peter 1:23).

The Word of God sustains life. Jesus said, "Man shall not live by bread alone, but by every word that proceedeth out of the mouth of God" (Matthew 4:4). Peter tells us, "As newborn babes, desire the sincere milk of the word, that ye may grow thereby" (1 Peter 2:2).

The Word of God protects life. Christ said that the thief, the enemy, comes only to kill and to destroy. This is characteristic of the devil. How can we be protected? By using the "sword of the Spirit, which is the word of God" (Ephesians 6:17). This is the sword that Jesus used on the

Mount of Temptation. He defeated Satan with "It is written"! The devil will try to make us doubt that God will heal us. Quote the Scriptures to him! Tell him, "It is written."

The Word of God inspires faith. "Faith cometh by hearing, and hearing by the word of God" (Romans 10:17). P.C. Nelson told me that at the time he was having his greatest success in praying for the sick he was constantly reading and rereading all the cases of healing in the Bible and especially those recorded in the Gospels. This became so much a part of him that it seemed the most natural thing to expect God to do miracles when he prayed.

We do not doubt the power of theWord of God on the lips of Jesus Christ, but does the Word of God when spoken by His followers also have healing power? It is interesting to note that on a number of occasions there is no recorded prayer or supplication, but rather a word of command given to the sick. In the first recorded miracle of healing after the Day of Pentecost, Peter told the lame man, "Silver and gold have I none; but such as I have give I thee: In the name of Jesus Christ of Nazareth rise up and walk" (Acts 3:6). Had not Christ told them: "Heal the sick" (Matthew 10:8, the Twelve; and Luke 10:9, the Seventy)? They were simply doing what the Lord told them to do.

Prayer seemed to be a spiritual preparation for the person who then spoke the word with authority. For example, in Acts 9:40 we find that Peter knelt and prayed and then turned toward the body of the dead Tabitha and said, "Tabitha, arise," and she did. In the same chapter the story is told of Aeneas, who had been paralyzed and bedfast for 8 years. "And Peter said unto him, Aeneas, Jesus Christ maketh thee whole: arise, and make thy bed. And he arose immediately" (Acts 9:34). Paul had similar experiences. In Lystra he found a man who had been crippled all his life and had never walked. Paul saw that the man had faith to be healed and simply spoke to him in the power of the Spirit, "Stand upright on thy feet. And he leaped and walked" (Acts 14:10).

These and similar incidents seem to indicate that the

Word of God on the lips of any Spirit-filled believer today would bring the same kind of results.

Besides the spoken Word of God and the written Word of God there is also the indwelling Word of God. Jesus told His followers: "If ye abide in me, and my words abide in you, ye shall ask what ye will, and it shall be done unto you" (John 15:7). How does the Word abide in a person? Just as the food we eat is assimilated and becomes a part of us, so we must feed continually upon the Word of God for our spiritual nourishment. We do not live by bread alone. We must have food for our souls. Regular eating habits are good for this purpose. Again, we should not "gulp our food down" but meditate, assimilate, until God's Word becomes a part of us. "Ask what ye will" certainly can include healing for the body. May God's Word abide in us mightily so we may not be spiritual weaklings, but "strong in the Lord," ready to do battle with the enemy and achieve great victories for our conquering Christ!

Remember that the Word of the Lord does bring healing. "He sent His Word and healed." "Speak the Word only and my servant shall be healed." Many evangelists testify to the fact that tremendous healings have taken place in their services while they were preaching the Word on healing, before they began to pray for the sick. I, too, have seen this happen. In the early days of the healing revival, many evangelists insisted that those who wanted prayer for healing should attend a number of services before they would be admitted into the prayer line. They felt it was very important to hear enough of God's Word to receive faith for healing and faith to retain the healing received.

How to Receive Healing Through the Word

Two things are necessary if we want to receive healing through the Word. First, we must know what the Word offers. It is impossible to have faith for the fulfillment of a promise if we do not know what the promise is. To claim the promise of the Word of God we must see what those promises are. Second, we must act upon His Word. Mental assent may be inactive, but real faith is always active. There is sufficient power in the promises of God, potentially, to save the entire world. However, that power becomes effective only as the individual hears and understands the promises and then appropriates them for himself and claims their benefits. In a similar manner, there is power in the Word of God to heal all sickness and all diseases, but that power becomes effective only as it is understood and appropriated. The Word must be acted upon!

God's Word is like its Giver—living, unchangeable, eternal. God honors His Word above His name (Psalm 138:2). He will do His part. He told Jeremiah, "I watch over my word to perform it" (Jeremiah 1:12, ASV). We must believe the Word. Faith is the key to all answered prayer and the Word will produce faith when rightly used. We must apply the Word. The Word is a cleansing agent for the soul. Christ said, "Now ye are clean through the word which I have spoken unto you" (John 15:3). This inner cleansing is most important and can be accomplished only through God's Word. We must use the Word. Know the promises and act upon them in faith. Resist the enemy with the Word. He will flee from such resistance when no other weapon will affect him. Finally, we must speak God's Word. Don't go around saying what the enemy has whispered in your ear. He is a liar. Believe what Christ says. Repeat what the Word of God says about your sickness. Accept the victory promised in His everlasting, unchanging, utterly dependable Word!

21

Healing Through the Name

A thorough study of the value and usage of the name of Jesus would doubtless revolutionize the ministry of clergy and laity alike today. The name was definitely associated with healing of sicknesses and deliverance from demon powers in the ministry of the early disciples of our Lord. In fact the Lord told His followers that certain signs would follow "them that believe," or "the believing ones." He told them: "*In my name* shall they cast out devils; . . . they shall lay hands on the sick, and they shall recover" (Mark 16:17, 18). The only Biblical prescription that we have for a sick believer states: "Let him call for the elders of the church; and let them pray over him, anointing him with oil *in the name* of the Lord" (James 5:14).

Significance of a Name

Let us first consider the significance of a name. In Biblical times a name was often an indication of the nature or character of the person. Jacob was given a name meaning supplanter or deceiver and so he was. God has revealed something of His nature and work by His redemptive names; thus Jehovah-Raapha, the Lord that healeth thee, becomes a title by which we know that He is interested in our physical well-being and able to do something about it. The name *Jesus* was not chosen by Joseph and Mary but was given by the angel that foretold His birth. There was a reason for the choice of this name.

Jesus is the Greek form of the Hebrew Joshua, meaning Saviour. The Lord Jesus Christ came to save from the worst enemy that ever afflicted mankind—sin and its consequences. The consequences of sin include sickness. We have already noted in chapter 1 that both the Hebrew and the Greek words for salvation include the ideas of deliverance, safety, preservation, healing, and soundness. Therefore, Jesus (Saviour) is our deliverer from both sin and sickness.

There are three ways by which a person may obtain a great name. He may inherit it, earn it, or have it conferred on him. There is no name on earth or in heaven greater than the name of Jesus Christ. The writer of the Epistle to the Hebrews tells us that Christ is the heir of all things, the One who made the worlds and upholds all things by the Word of His power; and, comparing Him with the angels, "He hath by inheritance obtained a more excellent name than they" (Hebrews 1:2-4). The fact that He lived a perfect life and purchased redemption for the human race certainly earned for Him the greatest name of all earthly heroes. Besides this God has conferred upon Him a name above all names. "Wherefore God also hath highly exalted him, and given him a name which is above every name: that at the name of Jesus every knee should bow, of things in heaven, and things in earth, and things under the earth; and that every tongue should confess that Jesus Christ is Lord, to the glory of God the Father" (Philippians 2:9-11). All creatures in three worlds or domains must acknowledge the absolute supremacy of that name! Angels, men, and demons must bow to His will.

This gives us some insight into the importance of the use of the name of Jesus.

The Right to Use the Name of Jesus

One of the great mysteries of grace is the fact that we have been given the use of the matchless name of Jesus! How does this come about? First, we are born into the family of God and therefore have a right to use the name. We "inherit" it, so to speak, when we are born of the Spirit, born again, and made partakers of the divine nature. Next, the right to use the name was conferred upon us by Jesus Christ himself. It is not an earned right, but one of pure grace.

One of the most astounding statements ever made by our Lord was: "If ye shall ask any thing in my name, I will do it" (John 14:14). This is the equivalent of a Power of Attorney. As superintendent of our church on a certain mission field I was given a general Power of Attorney to represent our church legally in whatever capacity the representation was needed. I had the right to buy, sell, or dispose of property and take care of other legal matters. No limitations were placed on this general Power of Attorney. This legal right was given only because it was felt that it would not be used for personal ends but only for the best interests of those who had extended me the privilege of being their representative. Surely the Lord wants us to use similar care with His name.

A lawyer was asked what the value of a Power of Attorney was. He replied that it depended on how much there was back of the name or firm that issued the Power. How much power, how much authority, is back of the name that we have been authorized to use? Jesus Christ had met and conquered man's greatest enemy. He had triumphed over death, hell, and the grave and was now ready for His victorious ascension into heaven when He told His followers: "All power is given unto me in heaven and in earth. Go ye therefore, . . . and, lo, I am with you alway" (Matthew 28:18-20). His authority and power are the greatest. They are supreme. As to His resources, " . . . all things were created by him, and for him" (Colossians 1:16). There is no limit to His wealth, His dominion, or His authority.

When His name is used by those that have a right to use it, it is as if the Lord himself were presenting the petition to the Father. He invites us to use His name; in fact, He seems to urge us to do so. He said, "Verily, verily, I say unto you, Whatsoever ye shall ask the Father in my name, he will give it you. Hitherto have ye asked nothing in my name: ask, and ye shall receive, that your joy may be full" (John 16:23, 24).

Jesus came to earth in His Father's name (John 5:43). He did His works in the name of the Father (John 10:25).

He sought the glory of His Father's name (12:28). He revealed or manifested His Father's name unto His own 17:6, 26).

He told His followers: "As my Father hath sent me, even so send I you" (20:21). His ministry was teaching, preaching, and healing (Matthew 9:35). Our ministry should be the same. He worked in the name of His Father. He has commissioned us to work in His name. As He sought the glory of the Father's name, so should we seek the glory of His name.

Early Church Used the Name of Jesus

Let us look at some of the examples of the use of the name of Jesus by His followers. When Jesus sent forth first the Twelve and then the Seventy to preach, He told them to heal the sick and cast out demons. How did it work? "And the seventy returned again with joy, saying, Lord, even the devils are subject unto us through thy name" (Luke 10:17). We have already noted that in the Great Commission believing ones were to heal the sick and cast out demons in the name of Jesus (Mark 16:16-18). They accepted the challenge, preached the Word, and the Lord confirmed the Word with signs following (Mark 16:20). This seems to be the God-given pattern that we should follow today. God will confirm His Word when it is preached on a subject. Where a "born-again" experience is not preached, people are not born again. Where holiness is not preached, people do not practice it. Where divine healing is not preached, there will be few if any healings taking place. If we want to see results, we must preach God's Word on the subject.

The first miracle after the Day of Pentecost shows us how the disciples used the name of Jesus and the results of its use. The story of the healing of the lame man at the Gate Beautiful of the temple is well known. The man was a beggar. He was over 40 years of age and had never walked in his life. Peter and John went up to the temple to pray and saw the man there begging. Peter told him: "Silver and gold have I none; but such as I have give I thee; In the name of Jesus Christ of Nazareth rise up and walk" (Acts 3:6). The man was then instantly healed, and he leaped, walked, and praised God. A crowd assembled and Peter took advantage of the opportunity to testify for Jesus Christ. First he denied that the healing was the result of any extraordinary power or holiness on their part (Acts 3:12). Then he told them how the man had been healed. Speaking of Jesus, the Prince of Life, he said, "And his name, through faith in his name, hath made this man strong, whom ye see and know: yea, the faith which is by him hath given him this perfect soundness in the presence of you all" (Acts 3:16).

A great multitude of people believed and accepted the Lord. This made the religious leaders angry and they had them put in jail. When they were brought to trial they were asked, "By what power, or by what name, have ye done this?" (Acts 4:7). Peter's answer was, "Be it known unto you all, and to all the people of Israel, that by the name of Jesus Christ of Nazareth, whom ye crucified, whom God raised from the dead, even by him doth this man stand here before you whole" (Acts 4:10). He even went on to say, "Neither is there salvation in any other: for there is none other name under heaven given among men, whereby we must be saved" (v. 12). Remember that salvation includes healing and soundness.

The religious leaders could not deny the miracle. Facts are stubborn things! They did not want this to continue, so they threatened them severely that they should not speak to anyone else or teach anymore in the name of Jesus. It seems that they did not mind their teaching new doctrines or a new religion. They were, however, afraid of the use of the powerful, miracle-working name of Jesus. The disciples were then released and gathered for a prayer meeting. They called the Lord's attention to the fact that they were being threatened. Then what did they pray for? It was a most remarkable prayer! They did not ask for protection or for the Lord to help them to escape. They said, "Grant unto thy servants, that with all boldness they may speak thy word, by stretching forth thine hand to heal; and that signs and wonders may be done by the name of thy holy child Jesus" (Acts 4:29, 30).

Note that they would be encouraged, given boldness, to continue by the continuation of the supernatural healings indicating the presence of the Lord. Also these wonders would be done *"in the name of . . . Jesus."* They were filled with the Holy Spirit and spoke the word of God with boldness. "And by the hands of the apostles were many signs and wonders wrought among the people. And believers were the more added to the Lord, multitudes both of men and women" (Acts 5:12, 14). Again the Jewish priests were angry with them, and bringing them to court they said, "Did not we straitly command you that ye should not teach in this name? and, behold, ye have filled Jerusalem with your doctrine" (Acts 5:28). This time they had them beaten and again commanded them not to speak in the name of Jesus. However, the disciples "daily in the temple, and in every house, ceased not to teach and preach Jesus Christ" (v. 42).

This account shows clearly that the use of the name of Jesus was a very important factor in miraculous healings and other wonders that promoted the extraordinary growth of the Early Church. They knew the value of the name. Even their enemies recognized the value of that name. They greatly feared its use, but could not stop it. Do we know the value of that name today? Is it being employed according to the Biblical pattern of the Early Church?

Jesus said that the "believing ones" would cast out demons in His name. This was done even before His death and resurrection, as we have already seen in Luke 10. We find another example of the power of His name to cast out demons in Acts 16. Paul and Silas were in Philippi for the purpose of preaching the gospel. This was the first missionary entrance into Europe. They were sure the Lord had sent them, but they had a problem. A young girl possessed by a spirit of divination followed them around for several days and kept shouting out, "These men are the servants of the most high God, which show unto us the way of salvation." Although what she said was true, we are not told how she said it. I can easily believe that it was with great derision and very possibly followed by sarcastic, derisive, demonic laughter. I cannot believe that a demon would be trying to help the cause of Christ! Paul got tired of this unsolicited advertising and, recog-

nizing the source, "turned and said to the spirit, I command thee in the name of Jesus Christ to come out of her.
And he came out the same hour" (Acts 16:18). The use of
the name of Jesus effected this deliverance from demon
power just as He said it would! Jesus kept His promise!
He always will!

We Need to Act in the Name of Jesus

We are no match for Satan in our own strength. The
seven sons of Sceva found this out to their sorrow. They
tried to exorcise demons, calling over the possessed persons in the name of the Lord Jesus, saying, "We adjure
you by Jesus whom Paul preacheth." They tried this in
one case and the demon answered, "Jesus I know, and
Paul I know; but who are ye? And the man in whom the
evil spirit was leaped on them, and overcame them, and
prevailed against them, so that they fled out of that house
naked and wounded. And this was known to all the Jews
and Greeks also dwelling at Ephesus; and fear fell on
them all, and the name of the Lord Jesus was magnified"
(Acts 19:13-17).

Not all have the right to use this matchless name. One
should be a true believer and be walking in obedience.
He should be filled with the Holy Spirit and seeking the
glory of God alone. If we meet these conditions, there is
no limit to the possibilities for glorifying His name and
spreading His kingdom. Did He not say, "Whatsoever ye
shall ask in my name, that will I do, that the Father may be
glorified in the Son" (John 14:13)?

Throughout the Book of Psalms we are exhorted to
praise and sing unto the name of the Lord. Psalm 96:8
tells us, "Give unto the Lord the glory due unto his
name." This can be done when we realize the worth of
the name and use it as the Early Church did. When we
begin to comprehend all that is included in the wonderful
name of Jesus we will echo the sentiment of the Psalmist
when he said, "They that know thy name will put their
trust in thee" (Psalm 9:10).

Many great names have been inscribed in the annals of
history, but the names of Caesar, Napoleon, Hitler, Mus-

solini, Stalin, and all the rest have lost their authority and power. People no longer tremble at their word. Their power was limited in time and space. The name of Jesus Christ is just as powerful and authoritative today as it was 1900 years ago. "Jesus Christ the same yesterday, and today, and for ever" (Hebrews 13:8). The inspired writer of the 135th Psalm cries out in admiration, "Thy name, O Lord, endureth for ever; and thy memorial, O Lord, throughout all generations" (v. 13). David expresses his feelings like this: "I will extol thee, my God, O King; and I will bless thy name for ever and ever. Every day will I bless thee; and I will praise thy name for ever and ever" (Psalm 145:1, 2).

May God help us to faithfully proclaim the name of our incomparable Saviour, Healer, and Deliverer, Jesus Christ!

22

Healing Through Faith

This remarkable statement was not made by some wild-eyed religious fanatic or irresponsible, ignorant person, but by the Lord Jesus himself, the all-knowing, all-powerful Christ! The One who has "all power . . . in heaven and in earth" (Matthew 28:18) states clearly that all things are possible through faith. Remember, also, that He was dealing with a case of physical healing when He made this astonishing declaration. The boy had suffered for a long while from something that resembled severe attacks of epilepsy caused by demon powers. The disciples tried to help and were unable to do so. The desperate father said to Jesus: "If thou canst do any thing, have compassion on us, and help us." Jesus replied, in effect, "It is not a matter of my power but of your faith." The father said, "Lord, I believe; help thou mine unbelief," and deliverance came (Mark 9:17-28)!

In words inspired by the Holy Spirit, James tells us: "The prayer of faith shall save the sick, and the Lord shall raise him up" (James 5:15). Just what is *faith* and how important is it in relation to healing? How can one pray this "prayer of faith" and get the desired results? Is faith a mystical power granted only to a privileged few or can every believer have faith? The volumes written on faith would doubtless fill a large library. We will not try to cover the entire subject but limit ourselves mainly to faith in Christ in relation to physical healing.

What Faith Is

Some seem to think that miracle-working faith is completely unobtainable for the ordinary Christian. They think of it as some type of semimagical element that cannot be defined and that is granted only to a few select persons. What does the Bible say about faith?

The Amplified Bible renders Hebrews 11:1 as follows: "Now faith is the assurance (the confirmation, the title deed) of the things [we] hope for, being the proof of things [we] do not see and the conviction of their reality—faith perceiving as real fact what is not revealed to the senses." Phillips states it thus: "Now faith means putting our full confidence in the things we hope for; it means being certain of things we cannot see."

Faith in Christ is confidence in Christ. It is believing that He is what He says He is, and will do what He says He will do. Faith is more than simple mental assent or belief. The devils (demons) believe that there is a God and tremble at the thought (James 2:19). Belief may be passive. Faith is always active. I once heard a fellow minister say: "Faith is the hand of the soul that reaches forth to God and never returns empty."

Salvation comes through faith. It is for "whosoever believeth in him" (John 3:16). (See also Ephesians 2:8, 9; Romans 1:16; 5:1; John 20:31; etc.) Since the very word *salvation* includes the idea of healing, it is logical to think that physical healing would come through faith.

Importance of Faith to Healing

Jesus often stressed the relationship betwen faith and healing. When the woman with the issue of blood pressed through the crowd to touch the hem of His garment, Jesus said to her, "Thy faith hath made thee whole" (Matthew 9:22). In the same chapter we read of two blind men coming to Jesus for healing. He asked them, "Believe ye that I am able to do this? They said unto him, Yea Lord." Then he touched their eyes and said, "According to your faith be it unto you," and they were healed. (See Matthew 9:28-30.)

In Mark 10:46-52 we read the case of blind Bartimeus, the beggar. When the Lord passed his way he did not ask for alms but sight. Jesus told him, "Thy faith hath made thee whole. And immediately he received his sight, and followed Jesus in the way" (v. 52).

In the case of the 10 lepers, the one who returned to give thanks and worshiped the Lord was told: "Arise, go thy way: thy faith hath made thee whole" (Luke 17:19).

When the Syrophoenician woman persisted in her petition for the healing of her daughter despite several rebuffs, the Lord told her, "O woman, great is they faith: be it unto thee even as thou wilt," and her daughter was healed instantly (Matthew 15:28).

The Roman centurion who sought healing for his servant demonstrated such faith that the Lord marveled and said He had not found so great faith in Israel (where the Word of God was known and taught). He then told the Roman officer, "Go thy way; and as thou hast believed, so be it done unto thee. And his servant was healed in the selfsame hour" (Matthew 8:13).

The classic passage on the limitless power of faith is found in Mark 11:22-24. "And Jesus answering saith unto them, Have faith in God. For verily I say unto you, That whosoever shall say unto this mountain, Be thou removed, and be thou cast into the sea; and shall not doubt in his heart, but shall believe that those things which he saith shall come to pass; he shall have whatsoever he saith. Therefore I say unto you, What things soever ye desire, when ye pray, believe that ye receive them, and ye shall have them." The unlimited scope of this promise certainly includes physical healing.

Hebrews 11 has been called the "Westminster Abbey of the Bible" because it contains an impressive list of the great heroes of the faith. Among the many exploits mentioned as having been accomplished through faith, we find that some were even raised from the dead (v. 35). This is the ultimate in physical healing!

Whose Faith Is Necessary?

Now that we have seen the importance of faith in receiving blessings from God, and how faith is directly connected with physical healing, we may well ask whose faith is necessary? Does the person prayed for always have to exercise faith? Is the faith of the one who prays sufficient?

In the cases mentioned above we have seen that the Lord often told the individual who sought aid, "Thy faith hath made thee whole." At other times He said, "According to your faith be it unto you." This and other such passages would indicate that faith on the part of the individual seeking healing brought about the desired results.

In the case of the Syrophoenician woman and that of the Roman centurion, their faith brought about the healing of a third party. In both of these cases the one for whom prayer was requested was not present but at some distance.

In the case of the palsied (paralytic) man who was brought to Jesus by four friends and let down through the roof because they couldn't get through the crowd, forgiveness and healing came when Jesus saw their faith. (See Mark 2:1-12.) Greek scholars tell us that "their faith" here refers both to the sick man and his friends that brought him.

Paul looked intently at a crippled man in Lystra and perceived that he had faith to be healed. The result? He commanded the man to stand up, and he leaped and walked. The people saw the miracle and wanted to worship Paul and Barnabas as gods. (See Acts 14:8-18.)

These passages all indicate faith on the part of the one prayed for or those who interceded on their behalf. Now let us look at some other passages.

Peter told the lame man, at the gate of the temple, "Silver and gold have I none; but such as I have give I thee: In the name of Jesus Christ of Nazareth rise up and walk" (Acts 3:6). Stephen was a man "full of faith and power" and did great wonders and miracles (Acts 6:8). Philip was used of God in a great salvation-healing campaign in Samaria (Acts 8:5-8). In Acts 19:11 we are informed that God performed special miracles by the hands of Paul. These references clearly indicate that the Lord gives special enablements, "gifts of healings" or the "gifts of faith" to some individuals and they are used to bring deliverance to multitudes.

The prescription given by James for the believer who is sick is as follows: "Is any sick among you? let him call for the elders of the church; and let them pray over him, anointing him with oil in the name of the Lord: and the prayer of faith shall save the sick, and the Lord shall raise him up; and if he have committed sins, they shall be forgiven him" (James 5:14, 15). This indicates that the elders should be able to pray the "prayer of faith" that brings deliverance to the sick.

Undoubtedly some individuals are used of God in praying for the sick more than others. Nevertheless we must conclude that it does not always matter who has the faith: the person prayed for, the one who requests prayer for the sick one, the elders of the church, or the evangelist or minister. Where true faith is manifested God answers prayer! The Lord's promise, "They shall lay hands on the sick, and they shall recover," was given to "them that believe" (Mark 16:17, 18). You do not have to be a fully accredited minister of the gospel or even an elder in the church to believe. Many remarkable healings have occurred as a result of two or three believers agreeing in prayer for healing or deliverance. Jesus said, "If two of you shall agree on earth as touching any thing that they shall ask, it shall be done for them of my Father which is in heaven" (Matthew 18:19).

How Is Faith Acquired?

Faith is not simply an acquired skill that one can master through courses of study. The primary source of faith is God himself. In Mark 11:22, where Jesus told His disciples, "Have faith in God," He was really saying, "Have the faith of God." God has given to every man a "measure of faith" (Romans 12:3). Without faith we cannot please God (Hebrews 11:6). We are to exercise our God-given ministries "according to the proportion of faith" (Romans 12:6). In our earthly race or warfare we are told to keep looking to Jesus "the author and finisher of our faith" (Hebrews 12:1, 2). Faith is one of the gifts of the Spirit (1 Corinthians 12) and also a fruit of the Spirit (Galatians

5:22). Thus the Father, the Son, and the Holy Spirit are all Sources of faith.

Dr. Charles Price in his book *The Real Faith* (see the bibliography) emphasizes the importance of having God impart special faith for miraculous results. One can have an absolute confidence, a full assurance, that this is the time and the place for his own personal miracle. This assurance is not based on any exterior evidence or sign, but on a deep-seated conviction that God has spoken and it will be done! It is the "faith of God." God is the source, and He imparts this faith without merit of our own.

Faith cannot be produced by our own initiative, but it can be strengthened and increased by certain measures. For example, we read in Romans 10:17: "So then faith cometh by hearing, and hearing by the word of God." Notice that it is not the Word alone, but the fact that God speaks. If a person is sure that God has spoken, he is not afraid to attempt the impossible.

Take a look at Elijah on Mount Carmel (1 Kings 18:20-40). Where did this solitary prophet of God get the courage to stand in front of the 450 prophets of Baal, the wicked king Ahab, and the vast crowd of assembled idol worshipers, and proceed with such confidence, believing that fire was going to come down from heaven on his sacrifice? His life certainly would not be worth much if that fire didn't fall! He had such assurance that he even made fun of those who were trusting in a dumb idol. The secret is found in his prayer in verse 36 where he says: "I have done all these things at thy word." God had spoken. Elijah heard and obeyed.

How does God speak? He has used many different methods in times past, but now speaks mainly through His Son, "the Word made flesh," and through the written Word, the Holy Bible. Faith is strengthened as we feed continually on the divinely inspired Word of God. There is no substitute for this food.

We cannot have faith to receive anything from God until we know what He is willing to do, what He has promised. This will has been revealed. We can know His will through His Word. One of the greatest men of faith this world has ever seen was George Muller of Bristol,

England. He fed up to 3,000 orphans and cared for them without any guarantee of support except the Word of God. He believed that it was wrong for him to even tell people of his needs, much less to ask for help! God never failed him.

How did he get such faith? He was a man of the Word. George Muller read the entire Bible through, with prayer and meditation, four times a year! The thousands of direct answers to prayer that he experienced are a source of amazement and strength to all Christians today who read the record. Faith comes through hearing the voice of the Lord, and the Lord generally speaks through His Word.

Smith Wigglesworth made it a rule of his life not to read any other book than the Bible, and God gave him a most remarkable ministry of healing through faith. You too can have "the faith of God."

Another means by which our faith is increased is through the exercise of the faith that we have. We are all familiar with the benefits of physical exercise. Paul Anderson was a weakly child. He claims it was only his mother's prayers that brought him through childhood. His doctor advised exercises to build up his health. He liked exercises so much and developed such strength that at the Olympics in Australia in 1956, he became World Champion Weight Lifter, lifting 1,175 pounds.

I once read that the ex-world champion heavyweight boxer, Jack Dempsey, developed such strength that he could deliver a punch of 900 pounds impact with only 6 inches draw. Exercise is all important to the athlete.

In a similar manner, our faith grows by exercise. David fought and killed a bear and a lion before he faced the giant Goliath. If you ask the Lord for faith, don't be surprised if He sends you trials and crises. He is giving you an opportunity to get the exercise needed to strengthen your faith. Don't shrink from an opportunity for development and increased usefulness for the Lord. God is glorified when we bring forth "much fruit" (John 15:8).

Demonstration of Faith

Real faith produces action. If you really believe a building is on fire you won't have to be urged and begged to leave. If you really believe God has healed you, you will stop acting like a sick person. James asks the question, "Now what use is it, my brothers, for a man to say he 'has faith' if his actions do not correspond with it? Could that sort of faith save anyone's soul?" (James 2:14, Phillips). He goes on to say, "Yes, faith without action is as dead as a body without a soul" (v. 26).

Elijah's faith was demonstrated by his actions. The same can be said of Moses at the Red Sea; Joshua at Jordan and at Jericho; Noah building the ark; Peter walking on the water; and every real hero of faith in the Bible. They got their orders, believed, and obeyed, and the miracle took place.

One of the greatest demonstrations of faith was that of Abraham. God had promised him a son and many descendants, yet the years were going by and nothing happened. Did Abraham doubt or give up altogether? Read Romans 4:20, 21. It tells us that Abraham "staggered not at the promise of God through unbelief; but was strong in faith, giving glory to God; and being fully persuaded, that what he had promised, he was able also to perform." Thank God for such an example!

In my mind I can picture Abraham coming out of his low black tent on a starry night, gazing up into the heavens and saying, "Glory to God! Thank you, Lord! You promised me that my descendants would be like the stars in the heavens for number! Thank you, Lord!" Why do I believe this? Because the Bible says he was "strong in faith, giving glory to God." Abraham's faith honored God, and God honored Abraham's faith. The same principle is true today. Faith honors God, and God honors faith.

Faith for What?

The faith of God for the will of God is our great need. Why do we wish to be healed? Are we thinking mainly of our own comfort and convenience or are we really concerned that God should be glorified? Do you think God would be interested in healing the arthritic hand of a pickpocket so he could better carry on his profession? Too many of our prayers are completely selfish. Our motives are very important. Remember that God looks right past the exterior and sees the very intent of our heart.

Another passage from James may be helpful here: "You don't get what you want because you don't ask God for it. And when you do ask he doesn't give it to you, for you ask in quite the wrong spirit—you want only to satisfy your own desires" (James 4:2, 3, Phillips). Let us always pray for the things that are according to His will. We can then be sure of an answer (1 John 5:14).

Faith in What?

The faith we need, the faith that glorifies God, is not faith in some evangelist or in a church or shrine. In fact some people seem to have faith in their own faith or in their lack of faith. We cannot by our efforts build up enough faith that will oblige God to do something. We need a little faith in a mighty God! We need faith in God himself, in His love, mercy, compassion, and faithfulness. We need faith in His power, authority, ability, and omnipresence. We need faith in His promises, His truthfulness, and dependability. The more you know Him the more you will trust Him, and this trust is faith. He is the Author of faith. He is the Perfector of faith. Let us ask Him, as did the disciples, "Lord, increase our faith" (Luke 17:5).

23

The Healing Power of Praise

Much has been said and written on the power of positive thinking. It is true that a person is greatly hindered by an attitude of continual negativism and doubts. It is also true that firm belief in your eventual success will carry you through many crises and greatly help you toward your goal in life.

Few people thought that Harry Truman was going to win the presidential election. He seemed very confident of the outcome, and win he did! But positive thinking alone, in the very nature of things, has its limits. Faith, God-given, Biblical faith, has infinite possibilities. Jesus said: "If thou canst believe, all things are possible to him that believeth" (Mark 9:23). Positive thinking can help even in physical illnesses, but faith in Christ is a much more powerful force.

Faith and pessimism do not go together. A person cannot have a real sincere faith in Christ and be pessimistic at the same time. It is like light and darkness—you have one or the other. Many times we would like to conceal our feelings from those around us, but consciously or unconsciously our true feelings come to the surface in our words, our speech. We may be able to persuade ourselves that we have genuine faith. However, our conversation will reveal whether or not we have that deep-settled conviction that God has definitely heard and answered our specific prayer.

Confess With the Mouth

Jesus said, "Out of the abundance of the heart the mouth speaketh" (Matthew 12:34). If it is football season, you do not have to be with a real football fan very long before he is talking football. He is full of it! This is why Jesus could say: "For by thy words thou shalt be justified, and by thy words thou shalt be condemned" (Matthew 12:37).

In view of these facts, it is easy to see why it is so important to speak the language of faith, and not that of skepticism, unbelief, and doubt. Our words are indicators of what is in our heart.

A very familiar Scripture passage says: "If thou shalt confess with thy mouth the Lord Jesus, and shalt believe in thine heart that God hath raised him from the dead, thou shalt be saved. For with the heart man believeth unto righteousness; and with the mouth confession is made unto salvation" (Romans 10:9, 10). Let us remember that "salvation" is for the body as well as for the soul. How do we get saved? Salvation is by grace through faith. There is no other way. A sincere heart-belief in Jesus Christ as the Son of God, the Saviour of the world, is essential to salvation.

But there is another condition. We must confess with our mouth. What does this mean? The meaning of the Greek word for confession seems to stem from two words that mean "speaking in agreement with another," "to say the same thing." In confessing Christ as our Saviour we are saying what He says about our salvation. He says that those who believe on Him will have everlasting life. We agree to this and witness to the world that we have everlasting life. It is a life that is new, changed, different. We become partakers of the divine nature. Christ is eternal and His life can have no end. He imparts that life to us, a life whose very nature is eternal! Thank God!

The expression "confession is made unto salvation" indicates that confession must come first and then possession. We confess our belief, our faith, in our Redeemer, His promises, His ability to save, and His finished work. Then we become possessors of the life that He alone can give—life eternal.

The physical benefits of health and healing, which are included in our salvation, are secured in the same manner. We believe, accept, confess, and receive. In both cases there may be no immediate feeling. We accept by faith, confess what God says about our sin or sickness, and receive the blessing.

It is at this critical juncture that many lose the blessing God intends them to have. They go by the evidence of their senses rather than by what God says. The devil tries to keep us from every blessing he possibly can. He is mean! Someone has remarked that if he were not bad, he would not be a good devil! Soon after we are prayed for he may try to bring back symptoms of our old trouble. This is when our confession is very important. Many will say, "Well, I thought I was healed, but I guess I'm not. I can feel those same old pains again." What is happening? They are not saying what God says. God's Word says that by Jesus' stripes we were healed (1 Peter 2:24).

What are we going to believe—the evidence of our senses or God's eternal Word? the voice of the enemy or that of Jesus Christ? The devil is a liar. He always has been and always will be (John 8:44). There is a proverb in Spanish that says: "En la boca de mentiroso, la verdad se hace dudosa." (In the mouth of a liar, truth becomes doubtful.) Will we believe what that old liar, Satan, says instead of the word of the One who says, "I am . . . the truth"?

The more we state our doubts, the stronger they become. We must take a positive stand. Confess what God says and faith will bring reality.

After 20 years of physical illness, Dr. A. B. Simpson accepted Christ as his Healer. He found it necessary to confess (to say what God said about his infirmity) before receiving the full blessing. Here are his words:

God did not ask me to testify of my feelings or experiences, but of Jesus and His faithfulness. And I am sure He calls all who trust Him to testify before they experience His full blessing. I believe I should have lost my healing if I had waited until I felt it. I have since known hundreds to fail just at this point.[1]

His healing was complete, and he was able to do four times as much work as before, and that without fatigue.

The language of faith will not express doubt, fear, or reservations, but will rejoice in Jesus' finished work and in anticipation of the promised victory. This is our confession. The possession will come.

Victory Through Praise

"Believing, ye rejoice." If we receive a *bona fide* offer of something good, we do not wait until we receive the thing offered to be happy about it. We rejoice as soon as we receive and believe the offer.

Praise has been called "the language of faith." Abraham was "strong in faith, giving glory to God" long before he received the promised blessing. It was a long, long wait, but he did not waver. He knew that God was able to do all He had promised, so he confidently awaited God's time. He was so confident that he kept praising God for the promise until the fulfillment came—about 25 years after the promise!

In contrast to this, we so often give up hope if the answer does not come within a few hours or a few days. God is not always in as big a hurry as we are. Let us await His time while praising Him for the victory promised which will be ours!

Agnes Sanford believes that we should visualize in our mind's eye the victory we wish to achieve or the healthy person we wish to be, and then thank God for the realization of our vision. As long as we concentrate on what we lack, the symptoms that remain and our lack of faith, doubts will increase and faith will be weakened. We should concentrate on how we are going to be when the work is completed, and thank God for what He has done, is doing, and will do. This will bring joy (which in itself is healing), strengthen our faith, and speed the complete victory.

Why is praise so essential to spiritual victories and answered prayer? The Bible tells us that God inhabits, dwells among, the praises of His people (Psalm 22:3). Heartfelt praise can, therefore, assure us of God's presence, and God's presence will assure victory. Let us look at some of the victories that have been won through praise.

Abraham has already been cited as one who praised God faithfully for years and then received the promised heir. When Joshua led the Children of Israel in their conquest of Canaan, they were faced with the walled city of Jericho. God gave them their instructions and they followed them to the letter. They did not storm the city or try to get in through subterfuge. They simply marched around it each day. Finally the day came when they were to take the city. The walls were just as high and just as strong as they were at the beginning, but they were told to give a great shout of victory while the walls were still standing. The priests blew their trumpets and the army shouted the victory. The walls fell down flat and the city was taken.

Remember that it did not matter to Joshua or his army how high the walls were or how strong. They were not going to have to tear them down. It did not even matter that there was no precedent in all military history to cause them to believe that the city's walls might be broken down by shouts and trumpet blasts! They simply obeyed God and left the miracle to Him. Doubtless they were mocked and derided by the defenders of the city, but they held their peace and did not shout until the proper time. The secret of their victory? "By faith the walls of Jericho fell down, after they were compassed about seven days" (Hebrews 11:30). Believe, obey, and then praise. This will bring the victory.

Undoubtedly, one of the most unusual battles ever fought is recorded in 2 Chronicles 20. King Jehoshaphat was told that a great army was coming against him. He called on all the people to fast and went to the temple to pray. He told the Lord, "We have no might against this great company that cometh against us; neither know we what to do: but our eyes are upon thee" (v. 12). A prophet then appeared and told them:

Be not afraid nor dismayed by reason of this great multitude; for the battle is not yours, but God's. . . . Stand ye still, and see the salvation of the Lord with you. . . . And Jehoshaphat bowed his head with his face to the ground: and all Judah and the inhabitants of Jerusalem fell before the Lord, worshipping the Lord. And the Levites . . . stood up to praise the Lord God of Israel with a loud voice on high (vv. 15-19).

They then appointed singers unto the Lord "that should praise the beauty of holiness, as they went out before the army." They were to say: "Praise the Lord; for his mercy endureth for ever." What was the result? "And when they began to sing and to praise, the Lord set ambushments against the children of Ammon, Moab, and mount Seir, which were come against Judah; and they were smitten" (vv. 21, 22). A tremendous victory was won through faith, obedience, and praise!

At the dedication of Solomon's Temple, all the Levites who were singers assembled, dressed in special white linen robes, having cymbals, psalteries, and harps to be used in their worship. There were also 120 priests who blew trumpets. The record says:

It came even to pass, as the trumpeters and singers were as one, to make one sound to be heard in praising and thanking the Lord; and when they lifted up their voice with the trumpets and cymbals and instruments of music, and praised the Lord, saying, For he is good; for his mercy endureth forever: that then the house was filled with a cloud, even the house of the Lord; so that the priests could not stand to minister by reason of the cloud: for the glory of the Lord had filled the house of God (2 Chronicles 5:13, 14).

It seems significant that the glory of the Lord came down and filled the temple while the people were praising the Lord. The times of greatest blessings in the church usually come when people lose sight of petty grievances and differences and begin to praise the Lord for what He is, and not merely for the blessings He might give.

The Psalmist gives us a description of how God works in the 107th Psalm:

Fools, because of their transgression, and because of their iniquities, are afflicted. Their soul abhorreth all manner of meat; and they draw near unto the gates of death. Then they cry unto the Lord in their trouble, and he saveth them out of their distresses. He sent his word, and healed them, and delivered them from their destructions. Oh that men would praise the Lord for his goodness, and for his wonderful works to the children of men! And let them sacrifice the sacrifices of thanksgiving, and declare his works with rejoicing (Psalm 107:17-22).

God does not require animal sacrifices of His people today, but the sacrifice of thanksgiving is always in order.

At the raising of Lazarus, Jesus stated a principle that is still valid today. He told Martha, "Said I not unto thee, that, if thou wouldest believe, thou shouldest see the glory of God?" (John 11:40). Believe, obey, and receive—this is God's order for the supernatural. It is well to note that the Lord gave thanks to God for hearing Him before He commanded Lazarus to come forth from the tomb. "And Jesus lifted up his eyes, and said, Father, I thank thee that thou hast heard me. And I knew that thou hearest me always: but because of the people which stand by I said it, that they may believe that thou hast sent me" (John 11:41, 42). He then spoke the command of faith and Lazarus, who had been dead 4 days, came forth alive.

Paul and Silas were on their first missionary journey to Europe. Because of the deliverance of a demon-possessed girl who was a fortune-teller, they were flogged publicly and then thrown into jail, their feet being fastened with stocks. What would we do in a case like this? There seemed to be no griping and complaining, no blaming God for getting them into such a situation. "At midnight Paul and Silas prayed, and sang praises unto God: and the prisoners heard them" (Acts 16:25). God, who inhabits the praises of His people, heard their praises and was pleased. He sent an earthquake that shook loose their bonds and set them free. That was not all. The Philippian jailor and all his household were converted to the Lord! Praising God in, and even for, all circumstances brings glorious victories that in turn glorify our Lord and Saviour.

Recent religious best-sellers on the subject of praise have stirred the Christian world to see the necessity for and blessings of praise. We urgently need to get to the place where we can comply with the Scripture passage that says: "In every thing give thanks: for this is the will of God in Christ Jesus concerning you" (1 Thessalonians 5:18). The basis for this acceptance of all things with gratitude is found in this statement: "And we know that all things work together for good to them that love God, to them who are the called according to his purpose" (Romans 8:28). It seems to me that this is an inspired truth that should be claimed and appropriated just the same as we appropriate other promises of the Bible. When the enemy brings to pass some evil or tragic thing, he does not intend it for our good. We can, however, claim the promise of the Word, and God will turn it to our good. If God can turn any and all the circumstances of our life to work out for our good and His glory, we can wholeheartedly thank Him for all things, regardless of how they may appear to us at the time. Trust in His divine wisdom and power, commit the matter to Him, and praise Him for the outcome.

A contemporary evangelist who has some extraordinary campaigns says, "Some of the mightiest miracles of healing that I have ever witnessed have taken place while the people were lifting their voices in praise and worship. The Healer visited His praising believers and healed them."[2] The experiences of many other evangelists and pastors confirm this observation. When we get our eyes on the Author of our faith, seeing His beauty, His holiness, and His power, we worship, praise, and adore Him not for what He gives, but because of what He is. Then He does great and mighty things. If we want victory, we must believe His promises and praise Him for the anticipated results, rejoicing with "joy unspeakable and full of glory."

24

Earnestly Contend for the Faith

Summing up some of the truths related to divine healing which we have considered, what is the practical application for today's Christian?

Those who are sick will find a Biblical basis for claiming the benefits provided through the atonement of our all-sufficient Christ. You should no longer be plagued by constant doubt as to whether God wants you to be well or not. Always remember that God is supernatural and it is easy, in fact normal, for Him to do the supernatural. He has revealed himself as the Healer of His people. He healed in Old Testament times; He healed in Jesus' time; He healed in the time of the apostles; and He heals today. Study the Word and follow the instructions carefully.

There were problems in the church at Corinth. The Christians there had come out of complete paganism. The city was noted for its moral corruption. Paul had to let them know that God has a purpose for our bodies that is higher than mere physical enjoyment. He wrote them: "The body is not meant for immorality but for the Lord, and the Lord is for the body" (1 Corinthians 6:13, Moffatt). Thank God that He is for our body! He is concerned and He can help, heal, strengthen, and make our bodies fit temples for the indwelling presence of His Spirit.

By the same token, we should realize that our body is for the Lord and let Him use it for His glory. We should offer Him our body, not as a burnt offering, but as a living sacrifice to carry out His plans, serve Him faithfully, and let Him love the world and do His works through us. "For ye are bought with a price: therefore glorify God in your body, and in your spirit, which are God's" (1 Corinthians 6:20). Your body belongs to God and He has a purpose for it. Cooperate with the Owner and keep your body in good shape so He may use it at any time. Glorify God in your body!

The very fact that our body is "programmed" for health, and not sickness, should be evidence enough that God wants us well. Paul prayed for the Thessalonians that their "whole spirit and soul and body be preserved blameless unto the coming of our Lord Jesus Christ" (1 Thessalonians 5:23). The Old Testament sacrifices were to be without blemish. If we are "living sacrifices" we too should be "blameless," whole, and healthy. If we are to serve the Lord, He prefers a servant who is well and strong.

As individual Christians we should be well acquainted with God's Word on this subject of healing and health, not only for our own benefit but to help others. In fact, the promised "signs" are to follow believers, not merely evangelists or elders. This is an important way in which we can help extend the kingdom of God. Many will be interested in salvation when they know that it includes healing for the body as well as healing for the soul.

Never forget that the real source of healing and health is the life of Christ within. "If ye abide in me, and my words abide in you, ye shall ask what ye will, and it shall be done unto you" (John 15:7). "And if the Spirit of Him who raised Jesus from the dead dwells within you, then He who raised Christ from the dead will also make your mortal bodies live by his indwelling Spirit in your lives" (Romans 8:11, Moffatt). While the world looks for better methods, God is looking for better men. "For the eyes of the Lord run to and fro throughout the whole earth, to show himself strong in the behalf of them whose heart is perfect toward him" (2 Chronicles 16:9). A. J. Gordon reminds us that "it is apostolic men that make an apostolic age, not a certain date of Anno Domini."[1]

We must not only remember the importance of the Holy Spirit's ministry in the lives of Jesus and His followers, but also carefully consider the full implication of the command to "be filled with the Spirit" (Ephesians 5:18). Myer Pearlman wrote, "The demonstrated possibility of demon-possession argues for the possibility of possession by the Divine Spirit."[2] Instead of talking and thinking so much on demon power, let us concentrate on being God-possessed and Spirit-filled. We can then cause multitudes to see the glory and power of our Master. He has said, "Ye are my witnesses" (Isaiah 43:10). We are to declare His glory among the heathen, His wonders among all people (Psalm 96:3). Say with the Psalmist, "I shall not die, but live, and declare the works of the Lord" (Psalm 118:17). We are to make His way known upon earth, His saving health among all nations (Psalm 67:2). This is our task and our privilege. We are to receive power for this task through the infilling of the Holy Spirit (Acts 1:8), and boldness through the signs and wonders that will accompany our testimony. (See Acts 4:29-31.) Let us not fail to be the kind of witnesses that He expects of us. Let us come up to His highest expectations for our lives!

What is the purpose of healings and miracles? John the apostle wrote of many healings and supernatural things done by the Lord and said that the Lord did many other signs that were not recorded. He then explained the purpose of the recording of these wonders: "But these are written, that ye might believe that Jesus is the Christ, the Son of God; and that believing ye might have life through his name" (John 20:31). If the purpose of miracles is to bring people to accept Christ and thus receive eternal life, then we need miracles today!

"In Yule's Marco Polo it is recounted that the Great Khan thought Christianity a far better religion than his own, but he could not accept it for his people because the Christians could not do anything of a supernatural order."[3] Is our God impotent beside the heathen deities? "Where is the Lord God of Elijah?" (2 Kings 2:14). We have no right to expect people to believe our message if we do not believe our own message sufficiently to see the signs follow that the Lord promised would follow them that believe.

Genuine miracles are a special revelation of the presence and power of God. They prove His existence, presence, concern, and power. They are occasions on which God . . . shows to man that He is a living God, that He is still on the throne of the universe, and that He is sufficient for all of man's problems. If a miracle does not create this conviction concerning God, then it is probably not a genuine miracle.[4]

There is no scriptural support whatever for the dispensational theory that the "days of miracles are past." In fact, there seems to be evidence that there will be a renewal of supernatural manifestations as we draw near to the time of the Lord's return. The Antichrist, Satan's representative, will be able to do signs and lying wonders, thereby deceiving many people (2 Thessalonians 2:9; Matthew 24:11). But the Holy Spirit is to be poured out upon all flesh in the latter days (Joel 2:28). Judging from the results of the outpouring at Pentecost and on the Early Church, we can confidently expect the Holy Spirit to work in the same manner today. Many signs, wonders, and miracles will be done through His power.

Satan tenaciously opposes anything and everything that will help the cause of Christ. Healings and miracles were mightily used of God for the spread of the gospel during the first century. No wonder Satan has opposed the doctrine and caused so many to doubt the validity of the gospel of healing for our day!

The fact that atomic power was unknown for so many centuries did not mean such power did not exist. It simply had not been discovered yet. There is healing power in Christ that millions of people ignore today. The fact that even many theologians have not discovered this power in no way proves its nonexistence. Abundant proof can be furnished for those who are searching for the truth. We are "surrounded by a great cloud of witnesses." Study the Word on the subject. If the Word of God teaches that Jesus Christ is the same yesterday, today, and forever, let's believe it literally! If the Bible says we should pray for the sick, let's pray for the sick. If the Bible says signs shall follow them that believe, let's expect the signs to follow our ministry.

The Word of God exhorts us to "earnestly contend for

the faith which was once delivered unto the saints" (Jude 3). The word *faith* as employed here means "the sum of Christian belief, the teachings, or doctrines that they had received." Heresy was trying to get into the church. Doctrines were being contested. Doubtless the enemy was trying to get them to leave out some doctrines as no longer applicable to their day. Jude felt impelled to write and tell them to keep the faith, to hold fast the truths they had received. Moffatt's translation of the entire verse is as follows: "Beloved, my whole concern was to write to you on the subject of our common salvation, but I am forced to write you an appeal to defend the faith which has once for all been committed to the saints" (Jude 3, Moffatt).

Notice that the faith was given "once for all." It is changeless. Times may change and the application of the principles contained in our faith may vary, but it is the same doctrine and we have no right to change, add to, or omit any part of it.

We are told to "earnestly contend" for this faith. This clearly indicates that there is going to be a struggle, a fierce battle, to keep the faith. Satan will try to destroy it. He will do his best to get us to give up portions of the faith, with the excuse that this part is no longer needed. Don't give way to the devil! Resist him with the sword of the Spirit, the Word of God. Tell him, "It is written." Phillips translates "earnestly contend" as "put up a real fight" (Jude 3). Many people do not have the victory that God wants them to have because they don't "put up a real fight" for their rights and privileges as a child of God. This is warfare! Thousands of eternal souls are at stake. Whether or not you "put up a real fight" for the faith that will attract multitudes and cause them to turn to Christ, may be the deciding factor.

This is not a battle for the weak! We are told: "Be strong in the Lord, and in the power of his might" (Ephesians 6:10). It is His strength, His might, that will enable us to be "more than conquerors" in this warfare. We are given the whole armor of God for our defense. The sword of the Spirit and prayer in the Spirit are our offensive weapons. Let us resolve to defend this faith and keep it pure, undiluted, powerful, and effective until Jesus comes!

Paul was a remarkably successful planter of churches. What was his secret? He kept the faith. He told the Corinthians, "And I, brethren, when I came to you, came not with excellency of speech or of wisdom, declaring unto you the testimony of God. And my speech and my preaching was not with enticing words of man's wisdom, but in demonstration of the Spirit and of power" (1 Corinthians 2:1, 4). Education, erudition, eloquence, and a pleasing personality may build a large following, but God help the church that is built on such a weak foundation!

Paul was well educated, and no doubt was capable of eloquence, but he wanted the converts to have faith in God rather than in his own personality or abilities. He demonstrated the power of God by the many healings and miracles that occurred in his ministry. It seems that this was done in such a way that the people knew that Paul did not have to be present for such things to happen. He doubtless taught that these signs should follow them that believe. Paul was able to say at the end of his most remarkable career: "I have fought a good fight, I have finished my course, I have kept the faith" (2 Timothy 4:7). May we do the same!

Jesus said, "I must work the works of him that sent me, while it is day: the night cometh, when no man can work" (John 9:4). All signs seem to indicate that the night spoken of here is approaching very swiftly. What we do should be done quickly. Jesus was asked: "What shall we do, that we might work the works of God? Jesus answered and said unto them, This is the work of God, that ye believe on him whom he hath sent" (John 6:28, 29). Hasn't He said that if we believe we shall see the glory of God? (John 11:40). Signs will follow the believing ones.

Jesus said: "As my Father hath sent me, even so send I you" (John 20:21). If we are to have the same type of ministry that our Lord had on earth, we will teach, preach, and heal (Matthew 9:35).

Do not think that because the time of the end is drawing near we will not be able to have any more great moves of the Spirit of God, revivals, and outstanding miracles. The prophet Daniel tells us that right up to the time of the Antichrist "the people that do know their God shall be strong, and do exploits" (Daniel 11:32). Take a firm stand on the promises of God and "put up a real fight" for the faith!

The Lord still challenges us with the promise: "Call unto me, and I will answer thee, and show thee great and mighty things, which thou knowest not" (Jeremiah 33:3). We have seen mighty things in the past. We have heard and known of many great things that we haven't actually seen. But the Lord still has some new things to show us, great things, mighty things! Let us accept the challenge and call upon Him.

Charles H. Spurgeon, a famous preacher and writer of the past—one who was called the "Prince of Preachers"—said,"The gospel is perfect in all its parts, and perfect as a whole; it is a crime to add to it, treason to alter it, and a felony to take from it."[5] Let us never be guilty of any of these crimes.

Paul was able to tell the Ephesian believers, "Let me say plainly that no man's blood can be laid at my door, for I didn't shrink from declaring all God's message to you" (Acts 20:26, 27, *Living Bible*).

Thank God for so great a salvation—one which meets every need of body, soul, and spirit!

Notes

CHAPTER 1

[1] C. I. Scofield, *Scofield Reference Bible* (New York: Oxford University Press, 1945), p. 1192.

CHAPTER 3

[1] William R.P. Emerson, M.D., "Health for the Having," *Reader's Digest*, May 1938, pp. 47-50.
[2] S.I. McMillen, M.D., *None of These Diseases* (Old Tappan, N.J.: Fleming H. Revell, Spire Books, 1970), p. 23.
[3] *U.S. News and World Report*, July 29, 1974, p. 43.
[4] McMillen, *op. cit.*, pp. 64, 65.

CHAPTER 4

[1] *Standard Dictionary of the English Language*, International Edition, (New York: Funk and Wagnalls, 1969).
[2] T.J. McCrossan, *Bodily Healing in the Atonement* (Seattle: Privately published by the author, 1930), pp. 34, 35.

CHAPTER 7

[1] Gerhard Uhlhorn, *Conflict of Christianity With Heathenism* (New York: Charles Scribner's Sons, 1894), p. 169.
[2] A.J. Gordon, *The Ministry of Healing* (Harrisburg, Pa.: Christian Publications), pp. 64, 65.
[3] J. Nelson Parr, *Divine Healing* (Springfield, Mo.: Gospel Publishing House, 1955), p. 70.
[4] Gordon, *op. cit.*, p. 59.

CHAPTER 8

[1] J. Gilchrist Lawson, *Deeper Experiences of Famous Christians* (Anderson, Ind.: Warner Press, 1911), pp. 376, 377.
[2] Gordon, *The Ministry of Healing*, p. 59.
[3] A. B. Simpson, *The Gospel of Healing* (Harrisburg, Pa: Christian Publications, 1915), pp. 154-174.
[4] Gordon F. Atter, *The Third Force* (Petersborough, Ont.: The College Press, 1965), p. 20.

CHAPTER 9

[1] E.S. Williams, *Systematic Theology*, Vol. III (Springfield, Mo.: Gospel Publishing House, 1953), p. 67.
[2] R.E. McAlister, *The Manifestations of the Spirit* (Toronto: Full Gospel Publishing House, n.d.), pp. 2, 3.
[3] Dennis and Rita Bennett, *The Holy Spirit and You* (Plainfield, N.J.: Logos International, 1971), p. 79.
[4] *The Reader's Digest Great Encyclopedic Dictionary* (Pleasantville, N.Y.: Reader's Digest Association, 1967), p. 864.

[5] Louis Berkhof, *Systematic Theology* (Grand Rapids: Wm. B. Eerdman's Publishing Co., 1972), p. 177.

[6] Harold Horton, *The Gifts of the Spirit* (London: F. J. Lamb Northcote Printing Works, 1934), pp. 111, 112. (U.S. edition now available from Gospel Publishing House.)

[7] A. J. Gordon, *Ministry of the Spirit* (Old Tappan, N.J.: Fleming H. Revell Co., 1894), p. 108.

[8] C.M. Ward, *To Another the Working of Miracles* (Springfield, Mo.: *Revivaltime*, Assemblies of God, 1969), p. 3.

CHAPTER 10

[1] Karl Menninger, M.D., *Whatever Became of Sin?* (New York: Hawthorn Books, Inc., 1974), p. 141.

[2] *World Almanac and Book of Facts* (New York: Newspaper Enterprise Association, Inc., 1974), p. 1030.

[3] McMillen, *None of These Diseases*, pp. 24, 25.

[4] *Ibid.*, p. 35.

[5] Gilbert Cant, "Your Aching Back," *Reader's Digest*, June 1974, p. 218.

[6] McMillen, *op. cit.*, p. 5.

CHAPTER 11

[1] F.F. Bosworth, *Christ the Healer* (Miami Beach: Privately published by the author, 1948), p. 54.

[2] A.B. Simpson, *The Lord for the Body* (Harrisburg, Pa.: Christian Publications, 1959), p. 14.

[3] Thomas Holdcroft, *Divine Healing, A Comparative Study* (Springfield, Mo.: Gospel Publishing House, 1967), p. 36.

CHAPTER 12

[1] J. Robertson McQuilken, (Columbia, S.C.: From a circular letter of May 1, 1973).

CHAPTER 14

[1] Merril F. Unger, *Biblical Demonology* (Wheaton: Scripture Press Publications, Inc., 1973), p. 61.

[2] John L. Nevius, *Demon Possession* (Grand Rapids: Kregel Publications, reprint from 1894 edition).

[3] *Demon Experiences in Many Lands* (Chicago: Moody Press, 1960).

[4] Lester Sumrall, *The True Story of Clarita Villanueva* (South Bend, Ind.: Published by the author, 1955).

CHAPTER 15

[1] David Womack, *Breaking the Stained Glass Barrier* (New York: Harper and Row, 1973), p.65.

[2] Louie W. Stokes, *The Pentecostal Movement in Argentina* (Buenos Aires: Published by the author, n.d.), p.24.

CHAPTER 16

[1] Gordon, *Ministry of Healing*, p. 120.

[2] Parr, *Divine Healing*, p. 35.

[3] Francis MacNutt, O.P., *Healing* (Notre Dame: Ave Maria Press, 1974), p. 9.

[4] Stanley M. Horton, *Into All Truth* (Springfield Mo.: Gospel Publishing House, 1955), pp. 72, 73.

CHAPTER 17

[1] *World Almanac*, 1975, p. 88.
[2] William Standish Reed, "Developments in Christian Healing," *Christianity Today*, January 30, 1961, p. 13.
[3] Simpson, *Gospel of Healing*, p. 183.

CHAPTER 18

[1] Nicky Cruz and Jamie Buckingham, *Run Baby Run* (Plainfield, N.J.: Logos, International, 1969).
[2] *Ibid.*, p. 13.

CHAPTER 19

[1] *Reader's Digest Almanac and Year Book* (Pleasantville, N.Y.: Reader's Digest Association, 1973), p. 860.
[2] John Lancaster, *Paraclete* (Springfield, Mo.: Assemblies of God, Vol. 5, No. 2, Spring 1971), p. 3.
[3] Gordon, *Ministry of the Spirit*, p. 82
[4] George Ricker Berry, *The Interlinear Literal Translation of the Greek New Testament* (Chicago: Handy Book Co., 1897), p. 417.
[5] James Strong, *Exhaustive Concordance of the Bible* (Nashville: Abingdon Press, 1958), p. 35 of the Greek Dictionary of the New Testament.
[6] George Jeffreys, *Healing Rays* (London: Elim Publishing Co., Ltd., 1935), pp. 55-57.
[7] Smith Wigglesworth, *Ever Increasing Faith* (Springfield, Mo.: Gospel Publishing House, rev. 1972), p. 151.

CHAPTER 23

[1] Simpson, *The Gospel of Healing*, p. 166.
[2] William Caldwell, *Meet the Healer* (Tulsa: Miracle Moments Evangelistic Association, 1965), p. 81.

CHAPTER 24

[1] Gordon, *Ministry of Healing*, p. 75.
[2] Myer Pearlman, *Knowing the Doctrines of the Bible* (Springfield, Mo.: Gospel Publishing House, 1937), p. 94.
[3] Charles J.E. Kingston, *Fulness of Power* (London: Victory Press, 1939), p. 8.
[4] Henry C. Thiessen, *Lectures in Systematic Theology* (Grand Rapids: Wm. B. Eerdmans Publishing Co., 1973), p. 36.
[5] C.H. Spurgeon, *The Treasury of David* (Grand Rapids: Zondervan Publishing House, 1973), Vol. Ia, p. 272.

Bibliography

Anderson, William Henry, Jr. "Sacramental Healing."
Christianity Today. January 30, 1961.

Armstrong, O. K. "Beware of Commercialized Faith
Healers." *Reader's Digest*. June 1971.

Atter, George F. *The Third Force*. Petersborough, On-
tario: The College Press, 1965.

Bennett, Dennis and Rita. *The Holy Spirit and You*.
Plainfield, N.J.: Logos International, 1971.

Berkhof, L. *Systematic Theology*. Grand Rapids: Wm. B.
Eerdmans Publishing Co., 1972.

Berry, George Ricker, Ph.D. *The Interlinear Literal
Translation of the Greek New Testament*. Chicago:
Handy Book Co., 1897.

Bosworth, F. F. *Christ the Healer*. Miami Beach: by the
author, 1948.

Caldwell, William. *Meet the Healer*. Tulsa: Miracle Moments Evangelistic Association, 1965.

Cant, Gilbert. "Your Aching Back." *Reader's Digest*.
June 1974.

Cruz, Nicky, and Jamie Buckingham. *Run Baby Run*.
Plainfield, N.J.: Logos International, 1969.

Demon Experiences in Many Lands. Chicago: Moody
Press, 1960.

Emerson, William R. P., M.D. "Health for the Having."
Reader's Digest. May 1938.

Gordon, A. J. *The Ministry of Healing*. Harrisburg, Pa.:
Christian Publications.

—————. *Ministry of the Spirit*. Old Tappan, N.J.:
Fleming H. Revell Co., 1894.

Grant, W. V. *Obsession and Oppression*. Dallas: by the author.

Holdcroft, Thomas. *Divine Healing, A Comparative Study*. Springfield, Mo.: Gospel Publishing House, 1967.

Horton, Harold. *The Gifts of the Spirit*. London: F. J. Lamb Northcote Printing Works, 1934. (U.S. edition available from Gospel Publishing House.)

Horton, Stanley M. *Into All Truth*. Springfield, Mo.: Gospel Publishing House, 1955.

Jeffery, Richard, and Mrs. R. E. Jeffery. *Fields Afire*. Dallas: Voice of Healing.

Jeffreys, George. *Healing Rays*. London: Elim Publishing Co., Ltd., 1935.

Jeter, H. P. "Power . . . Present to Heal." *Paraclete*, Vol. VIII (Winter, 1974).

Kingston, Charles J. E. *Fulness of Power*. London: Victory Press, 1939.

Lancaster, John. "The Ministry of 'Another Comforter.' " *Paraclete*, Vol. V (Spring, 1971).

Lawson, J. Gilchrist. *Deeper Experiences of Famous Christians*. Anderson, Indiana: Warner Press, 1911.

Lindsay, Gordon. *Bible Days Are Here Again*. Dallas: Voice of Healing Publication Co., 1949.

MacNutt, Francis O. P. *Healing*. Notre Dame: Ave Maria Press, 1974.

McAlister, R. E. *The Manifestations of the Spirit*. Toronto: Full Gospel Publishing House, n.d.

McCrossan, T. J. *Bodily Healing in the Atonement*. Seattle: by the author, 1930.

McMillen, S. I., M.D. *None of These Diseases*. Old Tappan, N.J.: Fleming H. Revell, Spire Books, 1970.

McQuilken, J. Robertson. Circular letter, May 1, 1973.

Menninger, Dr. Karl. *Whatever Became of Sin?* New York: Hawthorn Books, Inc., 1974.

Nelson, P. C. *Bible Doctrines*. Springfield, Mo.: Gospel Publishing House, 1962.

Nevius, John L. *Demon Possession*. Grand Rapids: Kregel Publications, reprint of 1894 edition.

Nuzum, Mrs. C. *The Life of Faith*. Springfield, Mo.: Gospel Publishing House, 1928.

Parr, J. Nelson. *Divine Healing*. Springfield, Mo.: Gospel Publishing House, 1955.

Pearlman, Myer. *Knowing the Doctrines of the Bible*. Springfield, Mo.: Gospel Publishing House, 1937.

Reader's Digest Almanac and Year Book. Pleasantville, N.Y.: Reader's Digest Association, 1973.

Reader's Digest Great Encyclopedic Dictionary. Pleasantville, N.Y.: Reader's Digest Association, 1967.

Reed, William Standish. "Developments in Christian Healing." *Christianity Today*. January 30, 1961.

Scofield, C. I. *Scofield Reference Bible*. New York: Oxford University Press, 1945.

Simpson, A. B. *The Gospel of Healing*. Harrisburg, Pa.: Christian Publications, 1915.

—————————. *The Lord for the Body*. Harrisburg, Pa.: Christian Publications, 1959.

Spurgeon, C. H. *The Treasury of David*. Grand Rapids: Zondervan Publishing House, 1973 ed., Vol. Ia.

Standard Dictionary of the English Language, International Edition. New York: Funk and Wagnalls, 1969.

Stokes, Louie W. *The Pentecostal Movement in Argentina*. Buenos Aires: by the author.

Strong, James. *Exhaustive Concordance of the Bible*. Nashville: Abingdon Press, 1958.

Sumrall, Lester F. *All for Jesus: The Life of Wesley Rowland Steelberg*. Springfield, Mo.: Gospel Publishing House, 1955.

—————————. *The True Story of Clarita Villanueva*. South Bend, Indiana: by the author, 1955.

Thiessen, Henry C. *Lectures in Systematic Theology*. Grand Rapids: Wm. B. Eerdmans Publishing Co., 1973.

Unger, Merril F. *Biblical Demonology*. Wheaton, Ill.: Scripture Press Publications, Inc. 1973.

Uhlhorn, Gerhard. *Conflict of Christianity With Heathenism*. New York: Charles Scribner's Sons, 1894.

U.S. News and World Report. Washington, D.C.: U.S. News & World Report, Inc., July 29, 1974.

Wagner, Peter. *Look Out! The Pentecostals Are Coming.* Carol Stream, Illinois: Creation House, 1973.

Ward, C. M. *To Another the Working of Miracles.* Springfield, Mo.: *Revivaltime,* Assemblies of God, 1969.

Wigglesworth, Smith. *Ever Increasing Faith.* Springfield, Mo.: Gospel Publishing House, rev. 1972.

Williams, E. S. *Systematic Theology Vol. III.* Springfield, Mo.: Gospel Publishing House, 1953.

Womack, David. *Breaking the Stained Glass Barrier.* New York: Harper and Row, 1973.

World Almanac and Book of Facts. New York: Newspaper Enterprise Association, Inc., 1974 and 1975 editions.

Index